C000080380

Nostalgic
Wigan

The publishers would like to thank the following companies for their support in the production of this book

A&P Cole Car Sales Ltd

R Banks & Son

Belmont Packaing

Edwards Funeral Directors

Sanko Gosei UK

Tim Calderbank Metal Recycling

Widdows Mason Solicitors

W M Edwards (Bakers)

First published in Great Britain by True North Books Limited
England HX3 6SN
01422 244555

Copyright © True North Books Limited, 2010
www.truenorthbooks.com

All rights reserved. No part of this publication may be reproduced, stored in a retrieval system, or transmitted in any form, or by any means, electronic, mechanical, photocopy recording or otherwise without the prior permission in writing of the Copyright holders, nor be otherwise circulated in any form or binding or cover other than in which it is published and without a similar condition being imposed on the subsequent publisher.

ISBN 978 - 1906649661

Text, design and origination by True North Books
Printed and bound by The Charlesworth Group

Nostalgic Wigan

CONTENTS

INTRODUCTION

Such has been the popularity of our previous books on the Wigan area, that we have been encouraged to produce a new publication. Our books allow readers to walk on cobbled streets, browse in well known local shops of the period and revisit special events and occasions, without leaving the comfort of their favourite armchair.

'Change' is relentless and in some parts of the area the transformation will be more obvious than others. Wigan town centre and the roads around it have changed significantly from times gone by. Some of the older and architecturally impressive buildings have retained their originality on the outside, however, their uses have changed. Quite amazingly there were literally hundreds of pit shafts within a few miles of the town centre in the late 1800s, and not a single one exists today.

The title of this new book, 'Nostalgic Wigan', tells you all you need to know about what is captured within its pages. Turning over leaf after leaf will bring you to a treasure trove from the last century. Through the photographs, images and thoughtful text, the reader is taken on a steam train ride back through the mists of time to an age when dad could buy a suit at the Fifty Bob Tailor or mum nip into the Meadow Dairy for a pot of cream. We make no apologies for the fact that some of the photographs will be outside living memory because they will still be familiar to us. They may feature an event described to us by a close relative or they could feature historical landmarks such as bridges and buildings.

Whatever the view taken on the boundaries which separate 'history', 'nostalgia' or 'the present', we should all invest a little time occasionally to reflect on the past and the people and events which helped to shape life as we know it today.

Wigan has always been a vibrant northern town, buzzing with energy, but different episodes in its life can be seen here. So, think of youthful days dancing at the Casino or courting in the cinemas of old and be entertained again as we revisit nostalgic Wigan...Happy memories!

TEXT	ANDREW MITCHELL, TONY LAX, STEVE AINSWORTH
PHOTOGRAPH RESEARCH	TONY LAX
DESIGNER	SEAMUS MOLLOY
BUSINESS DEVELOPMENT EDITOR	PETER PREST

STREET SCENES

Below: The tram headed across the old Market Place as people leisurely strolled across the cobbled setts. The new form of public transport helped make Edwardian Wigan feel a more modern place. There was something very 20th century about travelling on an electrically powered mode of transport. Before the coming of the cables and tracks, we relied on the power of the horse or our own two feet to get around town and its outskirts. The public toilets on the left were also a reasonably recent facility and a sure sign that the authorities took our comfort seriously at the same time as providing a little bit of modesty and decency.

Right: The tram on Market Street in 1902 was one of the first of its type. It helped change the face of our town centre in that it pushed shoppers and pedestrians further and further off the road and onto the pavements. They were supposed to be there anyway, leaving room for horses and their carts, carriages and the like. But the arrival of the tram with its power cables and dedicated tracks meant that people had to avoid the traffic rather than the reverse. Still, such public transport was a boon. Cheap travel and speedy transport saved both time and cash.

Below: Row upon row of terraced houses, squashed together on streets that were almost interchangeable in their similarity. This is where the working classes made their homes, a century and more ago. They were difficult times, but these residents knew little better. At least they had coal to use as fuel to provide them with warmth and a means of cooking meals on open ranges. The gas lamp offered a small amount of illumination to light someone's way home on a dark night, while inside the houses people reached for candles to light their way across the back yard and down to the outside privy.

Above and right: The top picture shows an Edwardian Wallgate when the world was changing fast. Electricity on our streets, powering trams, and in the homes of the middle classes, providing light, made our forefathers feel really modern. All around them, motor cars began to appear on the highways, forcing the horses and carts to one side. Before too many years had passed, the noble steed would be almost entirely banished from daily life as a means of providing a power source for transport. Above our heads the first aeroplanes droned on a precarious passage, initially covering very short distances. It would not be until 1909 that Louis Bleriot would manage even what now seems as a first short hop across the English Channel. By the time of the lower photograph, we even had electricity powering our traffic controls and everyone had become quite blasé about cars, buses, lorries and the like. For younger readers puzzled by the 30/- marking on the right, this was not a reference to a shop or house number on Wallgate. It indicated the cost of a suit of men's clothes. The amount in question was 30 shillings or £1.50 in the financial language we have used since 1971. Before it became 'the tailor of taste', Burton's was also the '30 bob tailor'. Henry Price, one of its main rivals, traded as the '50 shilling tailor'

Left: Sandy Lane, in Skelmersdale, connects Ormskirk Road with Westgate. It is still a residential area, though not as quiet as it would appear to have been just after World War I when not a single motor car could be seen on its cobbled streets. It was then very much a mining town, with a significant number of its population having migrated from Wales in search of employment in the Lancashire Coalfield that extended from Stalybridge to Ormskirk.

The interesting aspect of this set of photographs is that they span a period of about three-quarters of a century in the 1900s. In each case, the photographer was perched high above the town centre looking across Market Place from a vantage point on the Parish Church clock tower. The person holding the camera and the make of the equipment may have changed over time, but the angle of shot in each case is virtually identical. The oldest image dates from c1930 and shows that, despite the greater reliance on the internal combustion engine, the good old horse still had its place, pulling the LMS parcel delivery van, just outside the Maypole dairy near Slater's Stores. In the distance, the smoking factory chimney is a reminder of industrial days that are now in the past. The photograph from 1948 illustrates that there was still a significant

sector of the town, just beyond Market Place, that was heavily used by residents of terraced housing that would be cleared in later decades. The face of the town centre was about to change as well, with scaffolding at some of the shop fronts. These included Lace and Company, a firm of ironmongers and cutlers based at 25 Market Place, claiming to have been in business since the early 1800s. The buildings are all still recognisable in the latest image that now shows pedestrianised areas that have a shopper-friendly appeal. Less appealing is the sight of high rise accommodation, car parks and the blight of soullessly designed retail units.

Above: Both the handsomely domed Municipal Building and the Technical College were built on Library Street around the turn into the last century. The latter building, a fine looking red brick and terracotta establishment, would later serve as the Town Hall. It had been erected where a row of old cottages once stood. It opened as a School of Mines, the second oldest of its type in the country.

Below: A common sight in any decade is children hanging around on street corners. After all these were our playgrounds where we had most fun. Everyone stayed in the locality playing football or skipping along the street. There was nothing sinister about a group of children hanging around together. Very rarely did kiddies cause trouble because they new full well of the

consequences; a clip round the ear or possibly something much worse if dad got hold of you.

Above: The single-decker tramcar was headed for Standish, the village on the A49 road to Chorley. Standishgate, the road down which we are looking, quite simply means the 'way to Standish'. The old English word 'gate' did not originally mean an entrance, but the road through it and beyond. The lady pushing her Edwardian version of a buggy or designer pram was passing the place where some of the crème de la crème of Wigan schoolgirls were once educated. Situated near Powell Street, close to St Mary and St John's RC Church, Notre Dame was a convent school where the nuns

reigned supreme. They stood no nonsense and put the fear of God into their charges, along with a good grounding in academic subjects. With it being a Catholic school, there was always a fair degree of instruction about goodness and the evils of sin, especially those most evil of things, namely boys. Girls regularly had their skirt lengths measured and instructed quite definitely that no young lady from a decent home would ever show as much leg as Siobhan McLoughlin was displaying. '. When the school closed in the mid 1970s it was yet another example of saying goodbye to an establishment that provided the sort of good, basic education that was going out of fashion. Nowadays, we are wishing for its return.

Above: A charming picture as these young girls pose for a photograph at the top of Stairey Brow, Upholland. The steep hill behind the girls leads down to Back Brow which comes out into Alma Hill, just below the Old 'Owd' Dog pub. Dating from around 1934 it could have been taken for a Hovis TV advertisement some 40 years later. The happy smiles on their faces did not necessarily mirror the times in which they lived. During the inter-war period Britain was faced with industrial problems. The basic industries of ship building, coal and textiles never recovered from the slump they were in and by 1930 over 2 million people in Britain were unemployed. These girls, however, would benefit from a steady improvement in the health of the population in the 1930s. There was a growing understanding of the importance of vitamins, proteins and minerals in the diet. At the time, the Government was not very active in trying to improve health through diet, but from 1934 about half the children in schools were receiving one third of a pint of milk, either free or at low cost.

Right: Standishgate has been a major part of the retail heart of Wigan for more years than any of us can recall. Its face may have changed, but the activity on the pavements and behind the shop fronts is just as fervent as ever it was. Looking down from Market Place, it is probably the late 1930s as the trams are no more. They disappeared at the start of the decade, though the tracks remain on the street. Millgate is off to the right. At 1 Standishgate, we are looking at the site of the former Royal Hotel that stood here until 1925, before being replaced by FW Woolworth. The Eagle and Child, the town's oldest pub stood there even earlier as it dated from 1619. Grand balls were once held at the Royal and were popular with the county set. It seems ironic that such a class of people frequented what became a store for the working classes with its cheap and cheerful goods.

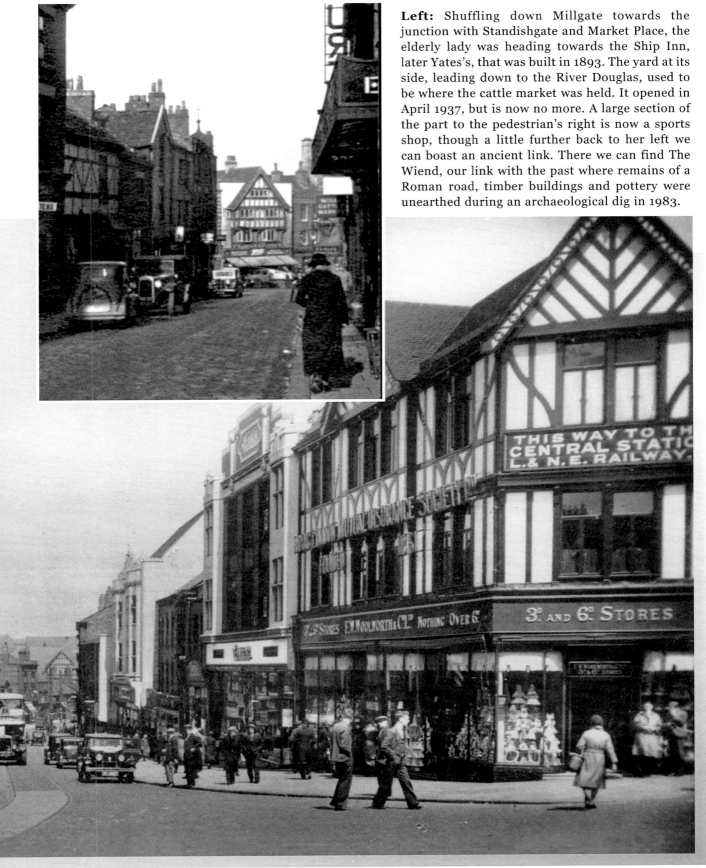

Left: Shuffling down Millgate towards the junction with Standishgate and Market Place, the elderly lady was heading towards the Ship Inn, later Yates's, that was built in 1893. The yard at its side, leading down to the River Douglas, used to be where the cattle market was held. It opened in April 1937, but is now no more. A large section of the part to the pedestrian's right is now a sports shop, though a little further back to her left we can boast an ancient link. There we can find The Wiend, our link with the past where remains of a Roman road, timber buildings and pottery were unearthed during an archaeological dig in 1983.

Gerard Street, Ashton in Makerfield, runs through the town as part of the A58 link with Bolton and Liverpool. The cables above the roadway were used by trolleybuses, known to some as the 'whispering death' as they crept up on the unwary who were crossing a road along which trams used to clank a warning. Their replacements were much quieter and could threaten the safety of pedestrians who were not watchful or listening properly. The town's economy was once heavily supported by the mining industry. Joe Gormley, President of the National Union of Mineworkers in the 1970s, was born here. In the late 19th century there were 13 collieries in the district, though a visitor could also observe a number of textile mills, potteries and factories turning out locks, hinges and nails. The Gerard Arms, over to the right, is a pub no more, becoming one of several bargain stores on and around this location earlier this century. Just further to its left, the Golden Lion continues to serve thirsty customers, though it now trades under the name of the Nags Head.

Below: Our gang was a real belter. We got together at weekends, in school holidays and in the evenings whenever we could. Our mums knew we were safe because we looked out for one another. There was little traffic on the streets in those days and you could hear a lorry coming miles away as it bounced along over the cobbled setts. We are not sure if the removal lorry in the background has any connection with Platt Bridge based Halls Removal & Storage, which was founded in 1921 by Mr Edward Hall a mobile greengrocer from Westhoughton. We went out playing games of marbles and conkers, depending upon the season, and kicked a ragged ball around pretending to be Dixie Dean or throwing ourselves around like Frank Swift at his best. Sometimes we just sat around, like little old men, according to mam.

Left: A very early picture of The Picturedrome Pavilion on Library Street in Wigan, claimed to be 'Home of the Great USA pictures'. The photograph is undated but the first 'Werewolf' film was a short silent movie, released by Universal Studios in 1913. Films could be viewed every evening from 8pm and Matinees ran at 2.30pm on three days per week. The Pavilion was demolished in 1959 to eventually make way for the new Wigan swimming baths, which opened in 1968. After 40 years the pool closed and was also raised to the ground, to make way for a state-of-the-art complex on the original site.

Below: Driving Lane ran parallel with the present Bridge Street, off Chapel Lane, at Pemberton, heading towards Wigan Pier. In the distance is a boat repair yard and the tall chimney of Trencherfield Mill looms above the housing that backs onto the Leeds-Liverpool Canal. Although the chimney was pulled down in the 1970s, the rest of the mill was retained and took on a new lease of life as part of the Wigan Pier redevelopment area. The smoking mill chimney, much shortened in 2005, belonged to Eckersley's and Western Mills owned the buildings to the left. Families with names that included Bretherton, Charnock, Lamb, Hickey, Dillon and Lowe lived in this location once over. They must have had a few problems with grimy specks on their clean washing. Perhaps they checked which way the wind was blowing before doing any pegging out. The canal was built during the 1770s, providing the textile centres in Yorkshire with an important link to Lancashire's major port and the world beyond the Mersey estuary. It also provided Liverpool with easy access to the coalfields to its east.

Right: Are these the Four Marys who featured in the Bunty from about 1958 onwards? Probably not, as we they are unlikely to have been members of the Third Form at St Elmo's, but they were obviously close pals. Skipping happily down Chancery Street, in Scholes, they did not have a care in the world. Oh, how we would all like to be back there with them. The world was a wonderful place to be when you were moving from the infants to the juniors. All you had to worry about was whether or not it was going to be that dreaded semolina for pudding again.

Below: As people boarded the bus near the toilets that once provided relief, quite literally, in Wigan centre, a cyclist and an officer of the law were deep in conversation. Once upon a time a policeman was allowed out on his own. You would be hard pushed to repeat this scene today. Before the humble bobby became part of the microchipped world, he was a real individual to whom we could speak. Those with a regular beat in the town centre were even known by name. He could be relied upon for a cheerful word and a bit of helpful advice if you asked him as he worked his way across Market Place. Our boy in blue was part of the community and we knew we could rely on him. Obviously an early photograph as ther eis no evidence of road markings and no specific crossing areas. The Belisha beacon, named after Leslie Hoar-Belisha, the Minister of Transport, was initially accompanied by a striped white line pattern on the road. These beacons spread quite slowly, it was the early 1940s before they arrived in Wigan.

This view was captured from the roof of the 'new' car park, looking down Chapel Lane. The main subjects of the photograph are the two cooling towers which were located at Westwood Power Station. The huge structures, each standing over 300 ft tall, were a well-known local landmark and could be seen from virtually every part of the town. The power station itself was constructed in 1950 but its useful life lasted less than forty years. Demolition of the cooling towers took place on Jan 5, 1989, and drew thousands of excited spectators to watch the event. Many people, particularly those who chose a vantage point a mile or two away from the towers, will recall the moment that the explosion took place; a cloud of smoke and a tremor could be detected at first, but no noise. Then, a tremendous explosion ripped through the air, causing photographers and observers alike to jump in the air with sheer surprise. The sound of cheering and applause followed, as the tension that had built up over the waiting minutes was released by the onlookers.

Above: The photograph, dating back to 1972, was taken from the top of the Council building, Crompton House. It shows Greenough Street, sweeping away to the left past the Upper Morris Street Working Men's Club towards the A49, Central Park Way. Most of the area has been redeveloped since this view was captured and the housing and streets to the right have a much more modern, if crowded, feel about them. It is still high density living, but with a brighter outlook. The building in the left foreground now includes a pre-school nursery. Some new names have sprung up on the road signs. The main access to the estate, leading from Greenough Street roughly where Vaughan Street once was, is now Sullivan Way. This thoroughfare is dedicated to the memory of one of the greats of rugby league. Jim Sullivan (1903-77) made his name as a teenager playing rugby union for Cardiff, the city of his birth. His talents soon came to the notice of those in the professional code and he signed for Wigan in 1921 for the then immense signing on fee of £750. He was the equivalent of a superstar in the nigh on 20 years he spent at Central Park, seen near the top of the photograph. He knew no equals as a fullback and his kicking prowess saw him break many records. He played 774 games for Wigan, scoring over 6,000 points, and represented Great Britain on 25 occasions. He managed and coached the club after the last war before taking on a similar role at St Helens in 1952.

Right: Wallgate in 1969, and a trusty Leyland double decker makes its way towards a point-duty policeman standing opposite Library Street. The

photograph seems quite modern, though it is over 30 years old and contains several interesting characteristics from the period. Among the retail premises the wholesale tobacconists business known as Ashton's can be seen, along with Howards, Johnston's the cleaners and the Wall Paper Stores next door.

LEISURE & PASTIMES

Designed by John McClean, Mesnes Park was opened in 1878; McClean was chosen to design the park through a competition. A rare aerial view shows the park in almost map-like detail, the main structure is the well used cafe on a slightly raised mound. To the left is the bandstand which has been the focus of so many concerts over the years. Rylands Mill is very prominent in the background. Also in the park is the statue of Sir Francis Sharp Powell, erected in 1910. A glorious summer day in Mesnes Park, was the setting for this delightful photograph (top right) which dates from 1925. The tree-covered river embankment can be seen in the distance, but all eyes and ears in this scene are focussed clearly on the music being played in the bandstand. Note the distinctive fashions from the time; the ladies look so stylish in their long coats and fancy hats, you can really feel the atmosphere of the day when you study the picture. The 30-acre Mesnes Park site receives two million visitors a year and hosts the Wigan One World Festival.

Above and below: The picture above of George Formby jnr, aged six, gives no insight into the fact that he would become a massive star of stage and screen by the 1930s. Formby was born at 3 Westminster Street, Wigan, as George Hoy Booth. He was the eldest of seven children having four sisters and two brothers. His father, himself a great music hall comedian, not wishing him to watch his performances,

moved the family to Atherton Road, in Hindley, and it was from there that Formby was apprenticed as a jockey when he was seven and rode his first professional race aged ten when he weighed under 4 stone. When his father died suddenly in 1921, encouraged by his mother and being too heavy to continue horse racing, he decided to follow in his father's footsteps.

By 1939, George Formby was the most popular and highest paid entertainer in the British Isles and was estimated to be earning over £100,000 a year. He died in hospital in March, 1961. He was buried in Warrington Cemetery in the family grave, and an estimated 100,000 mourners lined the streets on the day of the funeral to show their respect for one of the greatest entertainers this country has ever known. A bronze statue was unveiled in the Grand Arcade shopping centre on 15, September, 2007.

Above: A Norton International purchased new by comedian George Formby sold for £30,582 at an auction in December, 2007. The 1947, 490cc Norton International was one of many bikes owned by George Formby, who starred in the film 'No Limits', a spoof of the 1935 Isle of Man TT races.

Top right: Wigan was a hotbed for for rugged wrestlers, especially in the 1920s. These determined grapplers and seconds are at Springfield Park football ground before a match. Local champion at the time was Bob Silcock. Isaac Beech and Billy Riley were other well known names. The sport then lacked structure and two wrestlers could be locked in combat on a mat for hours. Although they attracted big crowds the bouts sometimes lasted for up to 50 rounds. The introduction of the more recognisable all-in wrestling in 1930, created timed rounds with victory obtained by two falls, two submissions or a knockout.

Below: The tagline on this picture could be 'Have books, will travel' or perhaps 'Danielle Steele's on wheels'. Whatever description you give it, the mobile library service has given easy access to reading material for many people in remote parts of the borough. Smaller schools could also benefit from the mobile library as a lending service for both non-fiction and story books also operated. The first mobile libraries were converted single decker buses. This one can be seen appropriately parked outside the Pavilion in Library Street.

Above: At the start of World War two, rugby league suspended its season immediately, but the Challenge Cup took only a single year's break before restarting, on a limited basis and with the support of the authorities, as part of keeping up morale. In the first final after the Second World War had ended, people felt safe enough to travel to London to see Wigan play in the 1946 Challenge Cup final. Here we can see a group of Wigan fans in London before the game. Unfortunately, Wigan lost an exciting final to Wakefield 13-12. In the same final, the Lance Todd Trophy was introduced and awarded to the man of the match for the first time. The first winner of the trophy was Wakefield Trinity Centre, Billy Stott. Wigan are still the competition's most successful club, having appeared in 28 finals and winning 17 of them.

A bird's eye view of Central Park in 1938

Left: Eric Ashton of Wigan and GB fights for a loose ball with Australia's JW Raper during the third and deciding test at Central Park in the 1959 series. Australia won the first test at Station Road, Swinton, and GB the second, at Headingley. The final game was the 3rd test at Central Park in front of 26,089 cheering fans. The team included four Wigan players in the starting line up. Along with Eric Ashton MBE, there was Michael Sullivan, Dave Bolton and Brian McTigue. The GB team won a hard fought encounter 18-12 on 12 December, 1959. This was the last game for the Kangaroos before moving on to play in France and Italy. During the UK tour they played 24 games, including the test matches, with an aggregate attendance of 345,000 fans.... How things have changed!

The first professional football club in the town, Wigan Borough, was formed in 1920 and was one of the founder members of the Football League Third Division North in the 1921/22 season. The team was withdrawn from the league in the 1931 season. Wigan Athletic Football Club was formed in 1932 and was elected to the Football League in 1978. The club was promoted to the Premier League, where they have remained ever since, reaching the Football League Cup final in their first season. The football club has ground-shared with rugby league club Wigan Warriors at the DW Stadium since it opened in 1999, after 67 years playing at the Springfield Park stadium, which had been Wigan Borough's home. The old football stadium was redeveloped as a housing estate after Wigan Athletic relocated. Life at the JJB Stadium is a world away from the days before the move from Springfield Park. With a capacity of 4,000, one seated stand and bleak open terraces, Wigan's former home was not a place for the faint-hearted, either in the crowd or on the pitch.

Ahoy there me hearties, Shiver me timbers! or weigh anchor shipmates - just a sample of the nautical terms that could well have been used as these sailors from Wigan Boys Club approach dry land. Their destination is not specified, it could be up the river to Parbold, or more likely a lake at one of the 'away' camps. These early forays were the forerunners of such as Outward Bound

courses and the Duke of Edinburgh Award Scheme. A canal holiday barge had been acquired and named the 'Duke of Gloucester'. The Duke, Prince Henry, can be seen here in August 1937, getting on a barge which bares his name to inspect it. Crowds lined the banks cheering and waving. Several times a year it would sail to the far flung shores of North Wales and the Lake District. The log of 1938 records details of the annual camp being held in Bingley, Yorkshire. Quite what these intrepid explorers would have made of setting foot in the distant lands of the White Rose county is unclear, but undoubtably enjoyable. It must, however, have been a difficult and arduous voyage crossing the Pennines by canal, as the series of ladder locks would have taken a long time to negotiate. Still, these lads appear to be no worse for wear after their excursions, having built up a massive appetite, messing about on the river.

This page: The well dressed crowd look slightly apprehensive as they wait to enter the Princes Cinema in the 1940s. Not surprising as they are queueing to see a double bill of horror 'Dracula and Frankenstein'. The films were re-released together in 1938. Both films were originally released in 1931, with Bela Lugosi starring as Bram Stoker's Count Dracula and Boris Karloff played Frankenstein, in the film inspired by a Mary Shelley novel of the same name. During the 1940s, Dracula and the Frankenstein Monster began to appear together in movies such as House of Frankenstein (1944), House of Dracula (1945), and Abbott and Costello Meet Frankenstein (1948). The Princes Cinema, in Wallgate, pictured right, was officially opened in October 1935, in the presence of British film actress Anna Neagle. On her arrival at the cinema she was introduced to the Mayor, Councillor James Hall, who later declared the cinema open. After the event she went on to visit Wigan Infirmary. Neagle proved to be a box-office sensation in British films for over 25 years. She won several awards as Britain's favourite actress and biggest female box-office draw. Almost all of her films were produced and directed by Herbert Wilcox, whom she married in 1943. She was bestowed with the CBE in 1952, and, for her contributions to the theatre, Dame of the Order of the British Empire (DBE) in 1969. The first film shown at the Princes Cinema was 'The House of Rochchilds', featuring British actor George Arliss.

Right: A Walking Day was a regular annual event for many people, particularly in our part of the northwest of England. They were church parades, usually taking place around Whitsuntide, when congregations and flocks of parishioners could publicly demonstrate their faith. They still occur today, but not with such numbers of participants nor in as many towns and villages. The walks were especially popular with Catholic communities, being an open

sign of a belief that once suffered restriction and even persecution. These lads from Ince in the mid 1950s cared little for priests' hiding places and chalices kept under wraps. They were happy to show off smart clothes and hope that Uncle Joe would drop them a bob or two when they called round later.

Below: The North Ashton Carnival float was very up to date. The residents of Hawthorn Avenue got together in 1950 to put on a display on the wagon that carried them around the streets to the accompaniment of admiring comments. The National Health Service had only come into being in 1948 and its benefits for the baby boomer generation were being lauded here. Free orange juice for infants, cod liver oil (ugh!) to ward off colds and build strong bones, milk powders with properly balanced ingredients, the provision of corrective spectacles and help with dental treatment were all part of the new government's welfare plans. Some of the youngsters, Pam and Tony Wilde, Eileen Tatum, John and George Davies, Geoff and Val Williams, Barbara Cross and Evelyn and Molly Ainscough, later recalled the day when they were the centre of attention.

Right: It must have seemed inconceivable at the time when the Wigan Casino Soul Club first opened it's doors, on September 23, 1973, that it would eventually have over 100,000 members and would be voted the World's Best Venue in 1978, by America's Billboard Magazine, beating New York's Studio 54. The venue began as a dance hall called the Empress Ballroom around the time of the First World War. The man behind the idea for Wigan Casino was Russ Winstanley, a local man who had been playing Northern Soul to the locals via Russ' Everysound Disco at venues such as the Wigan Beer Keller and Wigan Rugby Club. As the club's reputation spread, youngsters from all over the UK regularly made the trek to "The Casino" to hear all the latest Northern Soul biggies of the time. Many famous soul performers appeared there, including Jackie Wilson, Edwin Starr and Junior Walker. Operating between 1973 and 1981, it was known as a primary venue for northern soul music and became the place

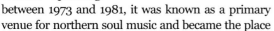

WIGAN CASINO SOUL CLUB
SATURDAY, SEPTEMBER 19th, 1981
12 Midnight to 9.00 a.m.

RETAIN THIS PORTION FOR DRAW
0743

END OF AN ERA - LAST NIGHTER
WITH THE COUNTRY'S No. 1 SOUL SPINNERS
RUSS, RICHARD, KEITH, DAVE, BRIAN, PAT, GARY,
KENNY, STUART & STE
9 NON-STOP HOURS ON TWO FLOORS
FREE DRAW AT 3.30 a.m.
FOR MUSIC CENTRE · T.V.'s, RADIOS, ETC.
FINAL OF DANCE COMPETITION
1st Prize - £100, 2nd Prize - £75, 3rd Prize - £25

EVERYONE WILL RECEIVE A FREE BADGE AND SOUVENIR POSTER

OLDIES ALL-NIGHT IN Mr. M's WITH KENNY, STUART, STE & BRIAN

Tickets £5.00 each   Members Only
Britain's Top D.J.'s, Management and Staff say goodbye to the Best Ever Venue and Most Loyal Supporters
THANKS FOR EIGHT INCREDIBLE YEARS

to be seen. A snapshot of this occurred in 1977 when 'This England', a TV documentary, was filmed and includes footage of the Casino over two nights in March of that year. The building on Station Road was demolished in 1983.

Right: Parbold lies in the valley of the River Douglas, which was canalised before the construction of the Leeds-Liverpool canal, the route of which follows the river up to Wigan. During the 18th and 19th centuries, coal was mined here and sandstone was also quarried. Both were exported via the Douglas and the canal; boat-building was also a minor economic activity. A familiar local scene is the old sail-less windmill, near the canal in the centre of the village. It replaced the water cornmill which once stood near the Douglas bridge in Alder Lane.. The windmill in its turn was superseded in the middle on the 18th century by the present mill which was originally worked by a steam engine and produced cattle foods until its closure in 1985. Visitors and residents can enjoy some lovely scenic walks in the area along a network of well-marked and maintained footpaths.

THE WAR YEARS

Below: A group of nurses from the London & Yorkshire Railway's ambulance train were pictured in 1917 on exhibition in Wigan. The ambulance trains performed a vital function during the First World War by tansporting the wounded back from the battlefields of Europe. By this time America had entered the war and the nurses carry Union Flags and 'Old Glory'

Top right and bottom right, facing page: The morning after the night before. Both images show bomb damage from air raids during the Second World War. It was reported that shortly after 10pm on 5 September, 1940, a German bomb destroyed the Independent Methodist Church in Greenhough Street (bottom right). Appalling though it was, apparently it could have been much worse, as earlier that evening choir practice had taken place and only minutes before the bomb fell several people had been playing table tennis in the church cellar. Not everyone who was out that night was teetotal and the good fortune extended to the pub at the

end of the street that was full of men enjoying a pint at the time of the bombing. Wigan was never a major target for the German bombers but nevertheless precautions had to be taken. Wardens, First Aid and demolition services were controlled from the Report and Control Centre situated underneath the Municipal Buildings. The personnel consisted of telephonists, shorthand-typists and volunteers, mostly from Local Government offices who took turns on the night shift and were 'called out' on sirens. Hag Fold estate (above), Atherton at Junction of Dorset Road and Car Bank Street, on 27th April 1941. The water main was broken, gas main also broke and was alight, Thankfully the damage was mainly to property, however many of the houses were damaged beyond repair.

Above: A group of ARP (Air Raid Precaution) 'Stretcher Squad' wardens rehearse medical procedures in the event of an air raid on Wigan. This picture was taken in November 1939, only two months after war was declared and at this stage they would have had little idea of what lay ahead.

Below and right: Two surprising images even in wartime. Large crowd gathered to see a captured German bomber and a tank from the First World War. When you realise the picture below is taken in the Market Square in Wigan, it is even more startling. The picture dates from 2 December, 1940. The massive aeroplane had been put on public view as part of a fund-raising campaign during War Weapons Week. War

Weapons Weeks were different from other war charities, as no money was paid by people to a named cause. This scheme encouraged a town's residents to save their money in various Government accounts, such as War Bonds, Savings Bonds, Defence Bonds and Savings Certificates. Cash would be paid into Post Offices or Banks. It would coincide with a week of parades, exhibitions and other war paraphernalia. Local residents would have the satisfaction that they had helped the war effort by doing little more than put some money into a savings bond. The backdrop to this scene is the imposing red brick building of O & C Rushton Ltd, better known to Wiganers, in later years, as the Gas Showrooms. Built in 1900 and extended in 1905, the Rushton building on Market Street, was originally a food and grain warehouse. The tank had an interesting role in the war. It was first used at the little know battle of Flers. It was then used with little success at the Battle of the Somme. Though the tank was highly unreliable - as

one would expect from a new machine - it did a great deal to end the horrors of trench warfare and brought back some mobility to the western front.

Above: Originally the Local Defence Volunteers, the Home Guard was largely manned by those who were too old to serve in the regular forces or were in reserved occupations. Wigan's representatives included some musicians who were able to put on a rousing concert in Mesnes Park in 1941. Augmented by a few young supporters, they played some stirring music that was meant to help stiffen the resolve of the locals as the nation tried to come through some of the darkest hours of the war. If German paratroopers ever descended from the skies, then these men were ready, willing and able to meet them head on.

Right: Pendlebury's clothing shop window was used on a number of occasions during the Second World War as an aid to the war effort. The owners were happy to remove the usual dummies and displays and allow the armed forces and civil defence units to encourage others to 'do their bit'. On this occasion, under the title of 'Made by men during training', we can see a collection of shells, bombs and bullets. This ordnance was displayed so that passers-by could appreciate that we were hitting back at the enemy and hitting back hard as well. Later, the ATS advertised for recruits via a display in this same window.

8th June, 1946

TO-DAY, AS WE CELEBRATE VICTORY, I send this personal message to you and all other boys and girls at school. For you have shared in the hardships and dangers of a total war and you have shared no less in the triumph of the Allied Nations.

I know you will always feel proud to belong to a country which was capable of such supreme effort; proud, too, of parents and elder brothers and sisters who by their courage, endurance and enterprise brought victory. May these qualities be yours as you grow up and join in the common effort to establish among the nations of the world unity and peace.

George R.I.

DISTRIBUTED in the SCHOOLS of the COUNTY BOROUGH of WIGAN

Left: This personal message dated 8 June, 1946, from King George VI, was sent to every pupil at Wigan's schools to mark the end of the Second World War. The King made a special wireless broadcast at the end of the War on Monday, 7 May, 1945, declaring that the day after would be VE Day, signifying victory in Europe. There had never been so many street parties – every road, avenue, drive and cul-de-sac treated its children to a feast. It was probably the first real party many youngsters had ever experienced. And from VE Day, the parties went on throughout the summer of 1945. Nowhere were the celebrations more vigorous than in Wigan. The Parish Church bells, which had been silent since 1939, rang out every hour on VE Day. The town was decked out in flags and bunting and there were fireworks and bonfires which lit up the night sky in a good way.

Below left: This photograph from 24 May, 1940, shows a group of refugees from Belgium and Holland passing the time by darning stockings and reading magazines at their billet in Wigan. On 22 May, the first wave of 171 Dutch refugees arrived in Wigan. The refugees told of their experience of being machine-gunned by German warplanes as they boarded their boat in Amsterdam. The boat was a small cargo vessel with accommodation for 50 persons, yet 270 people were crammed into every available space. All were weary and carried bundles of belongings or suitcases. They had come from an orphanage in Holland. The large crowd that met them at the entrance to Wallgate clapped and cheered when the refugees appeared. Having been bussed to The Drill Hall and fed, the visitors were taken to their temporary billets. They were housed in King Street Baptist School, King Street Methodist School and the Queen's Hall. The Women's Voluntary Services undertook the job of canvassing householders as to who would take in refugees either voluntarily, or for a billeting allowance.

Top right: The remarkable and heroic activities of Opera Star and local girl, Margery Booth, has emerged following the discovery of the only known photograph of her. She was born in Hodges Street, Wigan, in 1905 and joined the town's operatic society as a teenager. The family moved to Southport later, but she kept her links to Wigan, making her professional debut there at the Queen's Hall, on 4th October, 1935. Within a year she met and married German born Dr Egon Strohm. She went to live with him in

Germany and this ultimately led to her double life. Booth was sent to perform at a prisoner of war camp, Freigegeben Stalag IIID, where she met fellow spy John Brown. They became associates, both working for MI9, the intelligence branch who uncovered traitors. On one occasion after meeting with Brown, Booth performed at the Berlin Opera House in front of Hitler, with top secret documents hidden in her underwear. Margery never lost her patriotism, and after being uncovered as a spy, through her links to Brown, she was tortured by the Gestapo yet kept her silence. She was eventually released due to lack of evidence and luckily managed to escape during an air raid and fled to Bavaria. After the war she divorced her German husband and moved to America, where she died from cancer in 1952

Below: The war effectively ended when the cease fire came into effect on 15 August, and the surrender of Japan was officially signed on 2 September, 1945. This photograph shows a street party in Linden Avenue, Atherton, on 18 August, 1945. On the actual day trestle tables were set up down the centre of the road and covered with cloths. Chairs were brought out of the houses and arranged down each side. Use was now made of the precious items of food hoarded for just this purpose. Vases were filled with flowers picked from our gardens and set at intervals down the tables, which were soon laden with plates of food. Those readers of a certain age will have attended as children who went to the party with their brothers and sisters, and the babies were carried along too. Victory over Japan Day truly signalled the beginning of the end and people could look forward to seeing their loved ones again. This generation helped us be where we are today.

ROYAL VISITS

Below and right: A very special occasion from March 1945. Crowds of workers out in force to welcome King George VI and Queen Elizabeth to the works of Walker Brothers, Pagefield Ironworks in Wigan. Walker Brothers was one of Wigan's best known engineering works. The company is possibly best remembered for the manfucture of its mighty 'Indestructible Fan', used to ventilate coalmines across the globe. During the last war Walker's produced steam engines for use in both the merchant and Royal Navyl fleets, in addition to the production of thousands of artillery shells for the armoury. In honour of these efforts the King and Queen paid a visit to the works in 1945. Workers clamboured onto every vantage point to catch a glimpse of the royal couple as they toured the works. The vivacious and approachable Queen Elizabeth took centre stage whenever possible, as she knew her husband's failings as a public speaker. After the war, Walker's was taken over by Walmsley's of Bury, though the company name continued to be used. Subsequently in the 50s, the vehicle and mining elements of the business were wound up and the whole company finally closed in 1983.

Top right: This is an earlier picture of King George VI and Queen Elizabeth from May 1938, during a stop off in Wigan, as part of a much bigger 'Royal Tour of Lancashire'. and the St. John Ambulance Brigade. Their Majesties took every opportunity to meet people and can be seen here in Market Square greeting ex-servicemen.

The royal party entered the Borough at the boundary at Warrington Road, progressing through Skew Bridge, Newtown and along Wallgate, Market Street to Market Square. Market day had been brought forward to Thursday to make sure that the spacious Market Square would be available for the visit. School children were given a day's holiday, as were the Corporation's employees, and the Mayor appealed to local businessmen to make the same offer to their workers. As was usual on occasions such as this, a large parade was organised which involved members of the 5th Battalion, The Manchester Regiment, the British Legion

Glorious weather met the arrival of the royal couple when they visited Wigan on 21 October, 1954. The event was heralded as 'Wigan's Great Day' in the local press and it is estimated that 100,000 local people filled the streets. This was the first visit to the area of Her Majesty Queen Elizabeth II and H.R.H The Duke of Edinburgh and flag sellers and street vendors were out in force. The Queen looked a picture wearing a smoke-blue fitted A-line coat with an amethyst-sequined collar and matching hat. The Duke appeared sun-tanned and handsome in a dark grey lounge suit, with hands characteristically clasped behind his back as he walked, smiling through the happy, cheering Wigan crowds. People, young and old, had been waiting from early morning to catch a glimpse of the Royal visitors. The crowd was ten or twelve deep in places and were being controlled by hundreds of police, soldiers, and even fire brigade personnel. Office windows above street-level were crammed with eager faces, high, often precarious vantage points were scaled by the athletic and ingenious in order to find that ideal spot from which to secure an ideal view. Her Majesty's gleaming black Rolls Royce, plumed with the royal standard and supported by four other immaculately turned out vehicles, all travelling at a sedate two miles per hour was soon travelling to the John McCurdy Hall, and the main purpose of the

visit. The Hall had been opened at a cost of £220,000, with further additions planned which would bring the total up to more than a million pounds. Local dignitaries were introduced to the Queen and Prince Philip, and a special conversation took place with Cllr McCurdy, the hard working civic figure after whom the building had been named. A gold key was presented to the Queen who used it to open a door and formally declare the building open.

Top left and left: These two photographs from the 1950s show a very special visit to Wigan from Princess Margaret, who at the time time was third in line to the throne. Thousands of people lined the streets, anxious to catch a glimpse of the Queen's sister. She can be seen stepping out of the royal car outside the old Borough offices on the corner of King Street and Rodney Street. As usual on such occasions, the red carpet had been rolled out and the mayor and mayoress were on hand to greet the Princess. From 1952, when her father died, Princess Margaret took on more and more official duties as her sister's senior representative. With no widespread TV coverage in those days, the crowd strained to see someone so important in the flesh. It was a treat not to be missed. In the second image, Princess Margaret looks stunning dressed in the height of expensive fashion of the time.

Above: Wigan's fond connections with the Royal Family date back to the days of Henry III, who granted the town its Royal Charter. The Windsors made several visits to Wigan in the 1950s and Queen Elizabeth, the Queen Mother, can be seen here on one such visit. The crowd consisting mainly of women and children, watch on as she returns to her royal car on the corner of Rodney Street in 1954. The three lions shield is situated above her as she takes to the red carpet proudly rolled out in her honour. Looking down from this elevated vantage point we can see that at this time there was not the high level of security that would be essential today. Only four uniformed police officers are in shot to control events. During another royal visit in 1959 Queen Elizabeth visited the new H.J. Heinz factory at Kitt Green. A month earlier the factory had been opened by the Lord Chancellor, Viscount Kilmuir.

PEOPLE & PLACES

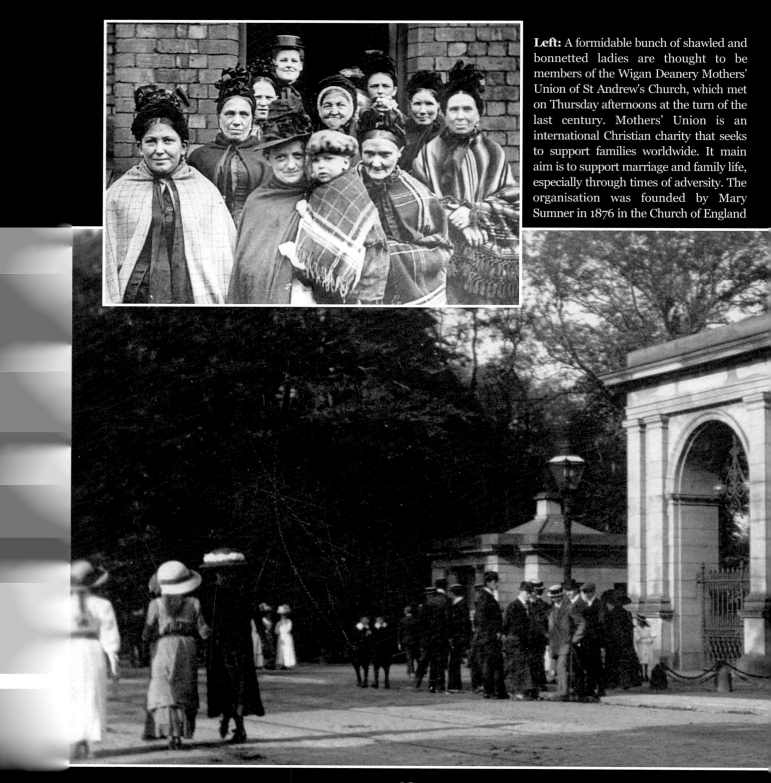

Left: A formidable bunch of shawled and bonnetted ladies are thought to be members of the Wigan Deanery Mothers' Union of St Andrew's Church, which met on Thursday afternoons at the turn of the last century. Mothers' Union is an international Christian charity that seeks to support families worldwide. It main aim is to support marriage and family life, especially through times of adversity. The organisation was founded by Mary Sumner in 1876 in the Church of England

parish of Old Alresford, near Winchester, where her husband was rector. She was inspired to start the movement after the birth of her first grandchild. Remembering her own difficulties when she was first a mother, Sumner wanted to bring mothers of all social classes together to provide support for one another and to be trained in motherhood, something which she saw as a vocation

Left: A well dressed group gather outside Plantation Gates, Wigan Lane. This is an early view of Plantation Gates, best described as a "Neo-classical gateway, with attached lodges of 1840, forming the approach to Haigh Hall from the south-west. The Plantation Gates are Grade II* listed, and currently one of four Wigan buildings on the 'English Heritage Buildings At Risk'. The stone was cut to shape on site and was also used for the rebuilding of the house. A landmark in the town of Wigan, the Earl certainly wanted to show off his estate and allowed the use of the Lower Plantations to the Wigan public all year round, except for one day of the year to preserve ownership rights.

Above: This picture shows the motor cavalcade of General Booth who founded the Salvation Army, as it travels along Market Street in August 1906. William Booth was born in Sneinton, Nottingham in 1829 and was a British Methodist Preacher who founded the Salvation Army and became its first General. His automobile campaign saw him travel from one end of England to the other (over 12,000 miles) by motorcar. Here he can be seen in the back seat of the second vehicle on his way through Wigan. During his lifetime Booth established Army work in 58 countries and colonies. He visited Wigan again in July,1911 as part of a second and final tour. He died a year later.

NOSTALGIC WIGAN

Right: The cobblestones of Market Square echo to the sound of hundreds of tiny feet lining up to get a small gift or sweets to mark a special day for the school children of Wigan. It's 1922 and Mayor Pagett has a treat for the kiddies. Those sorts of events have disappeared from our calendar, it seems. At one time, we were always receiving special presents or days off from school. When there was Royalty in town, we've get the chance to go and stand on the footpath lining the route. The teachers would have been surprised if the event had not been marked in such a way. Either the bishop or the mayor would come and visit the classrooms or attend Speech Day. Didn't he always ask the head to give us a half day, at least, to mark his visit? We all gave him three cheers for doing so. Goodness only knows what would have happened if the head had refused! Anarchy in the schoolroom, rebellion in the staffroom; where would it have all ended? No doubt with the National Curriculum, school league tables and inspectors closing down schools, but that's a debate for another time. Towering over the square is the centre of the Rushton empire and dates from 1905. Oates and George Rushton came to Wigan in 1870, setting up shop on Market Place. Eventually, they had 60 shops in the area. The business was sold in 1957.

Below: Famous 'Road to Wigan Pier' Auther, George Orwell, lodged above this corner shop in Wigan while researching his famous book. Orwell spent February, 1936, staying in dirty lodgings over a tripe shop. During his time in Wigan he gained entry to many houses to see how people lived, took systematic notes of housing conditions and wages earned, went down a coal mine, and spent days at the local public library consulting public health records and reports on working conditions in mines. This was a part of his investigation which gave rise to The Road to Wigan Pier, published a year later in 1937.

Below: The Parish Church of All Saints is the oldest church in Wigan and stands on the crest of a hill at the top of Crawford Street and Bishopgate. This picture was taken in 1901 looking at the church from Bishopgate. The church is medieval but most of the present building was erected between 1845 and 1850 by Edmund Sharpe and Edward Graham Paley, when it was almost entirely rebuilt at a cost of £15,000, which if repeated today would be in the region of 1.2 million. It was a copy of the Church which was taken down, which seems to have dated in the main from the later Middle Ages, though parts of the tower and perhaps other fragments were earlier..

Right: Even the scaffolding on the Parish Church cannot hide the imposing splendour of this beautiful and much loved building. You only have to gaze at the exterior to be struck by the enormous ability of the stonemasons who laboured to produce the architectural lines of the ancient tower and main body of the church itself. The original Gothic style was vaulted, that is, roofed with arching sheets of stone. By the 14th century most major European towns and cities had similarly styled churches.

This page: The Foundation Stone Of The Royal Albert Edward Infirmary was laid on Boxing Day 1870 and after completion was opened by the Prince of Wales in 1873. Albert Edward (pictured left) Prince of Wales (1841-1910), was the eldest son of Queen Victoria and Prince Albert and later King Edward VII. More commonly known to locals as Wigan Infirmary, the site on Wigan Lane, has been redeveloped over the years and now has over 500 beds.

Right: The Eight Lancashire Lads was a troupe of young male dancers who toured the music halls of Great Britain in the late 19th and early 20th centuries. They were founded by Bill Cawley and J.W. Jackson of Wigan. As they became more successful, they recruited other group members. The legendary Charlie Chaplin got his first professional break with them at the age of twelve. Coming from a family of great performers, his father was a versatile vocalist and actor and his mother, Hannah Chaplin, known under the stage name of Lily Harley, was an attractive actress and singer. The legendary Chaplin was born in London in 1889 and made his professional debut as a member of "The Eight Lancashire Lads" and rapidly won popular favour as an outstanding tap dancer.

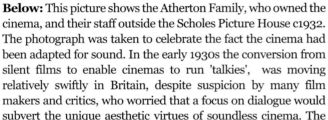

Below: This picture shows the Atherton Family, who owned the cinema, and their staff outside the Scholes Picture House c1932. The photograph was taken to celebrate the fact the cinema had been adapted for sound. In the early 1930s the conversion from silent films to enable cinemas to run 'talkies', was moving relatively swiftly in Britain, despite suspicion by many film makers and critics, who worried that a focus on dialogue would subvert the unique aesthetic virtues of soundless cinema. The first successful European dramatic talkie was the all-British Blackmail. Directed by twenty-nine-year-old Alfred Hitchcock, the movie had its London debut on June 21, 1929. Originally shot as a silent, Blackmail was restaged to include dialogue sequences, along with a score and sound effects, before its premiere. The posters show the latest offering, King of the Khyber Rifles, which was released in 1929 starring Victor McLaglen and Myrna Loy. The film was adapted from a novel by British writer Talbot Mundy.

Above: 'I won't take my coat off I'm not stopping', so said local Lancashire comic Ken Platt on the stage of the Grand Theatre and Hippodrome. Back in the late 1950s when this photograph was taken. He couldn't have stopped for long as it was badly damaged by fire in 1956 and demolished around 1960. From its opening in 1903, the 'Hipp' hosted many famous music hall and variety acts. Both George Formby Snr (left) and Jnr performed here, however, by the time of this picture the variety bill had run its course. TV was changing the way people were entertained and as the Frank H Fortesque Players, a professional rep company, headed by Arthur Leslie (Jack Walker of Coronation Street) gave a different play every week. Famous actor Sir Ian McKellen was a big fan in the 1940s, when he and his family lived within walking distance of the theatre. Even at the age of 10 he was an admirer of the actors who managed to present a new production each week. Colin Bean, who played Private Sponge in Dad's Army, lived in Wigan all his life and also started at the Hippodrome with walk-on parts for the Fortesque Players.

programmes like 'Sunday Night At The London Palladium' were growing audiences, the likes of the Hippodrome were closing. The theatre was on King Street opposite Rodney House.

Right: One of Lancashire's best known music halls was the Wigan Hippodrome, in King Street. It was damaged by fire in April, 1956. Eventually it was demolished and Lennon's Supermarket opened on the site. In the latter years, before closure,

Below: In 1867 Colonel Henry Blundell, the owner of the Pemberton Collieries, built the Pemberton Colliery Iron School Church which stood on the corner of Foundry Lane and Billinge Road. This building, along with a house for the Curate and another for the Schoolmaster, was the beginning of the many generous gifts which Colonel Henry Blundell made to St Matthew's, to provide education and spiritual teaching to his workers and their families as well as to anyone else in the area who came to the school and church. The photograph of the infants class was taken in the early part of the 20th century before the school was renamed as Highfield Junior Mixed.

Below and bottom right: Highfield Junior School, Class 3, 1956. Ron Hunt is pictured 4th from the left in the middle row. Our thanks go out to Ron who has been extremely helpful in the supply of photographs for this publication. A staunch Wigan football supporter there is not much he doesn't know about the area.

So small, yet so famous. It's actually a metal rail at the end of the tramway at Wigan's canal wharf. The original "pier" at Wigan was a coal loading staithe, probably a wooden jetty, where wagons from a nearby colliery were unloaded into waiting barges on the canal. The original wooden pier is believed to have been demolished in 1929. Its fame is thought to have originated as a music hall joke comparing it on favourable terms with the rather longer piers at Blackpool and Southport. And then, of course, George Orwell carried it on with his book 'The Road To Wigan Pier'. It is now a major tourist attraction in Wigan.

Left: A photo taken on the what is now Highfield cricket field. Girls from Highfield school dance at the Garden Fete in the mid-1950s.

Above and below: It is thought that the above picture dates from the early 1920s and shows the locks joining the Leeds and Liverpool Canal to the River Douglas at Gathurst. The lock keeper's cottage in the foreground is still there today. The bridge has been taken down and the area in the front of the picture is a basin on the canal. The house in the top left is part of Dean Cottages and has long since been demolished. The elevated view is looking north west from a high sloping field. If it was taken today the photographer would be up against the M6 northbound carriageway seen on the left.

Facing page: Wigan Central railway station was situated on Station Road, off Millgate. The station was built by the Manchester, Sheffield and Lincolnshire Railway (later to become the Great Central) and opened on 3 October, 1892. It replaced Wigan's Darlington Street station, which had opened on 1 April, 1884, on the extension of the line nearer to the town centre. Wigan Central was the terminus of the Wigan Junction Railways from Glazebrook Junction and closed to passengers on 2 November, 1964, although it was five months before the station closed completely. According to Beeching's reshaping of British Railways the line was more heavily used than many which did not

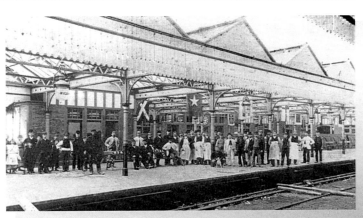

close; as with many unmodernised and heavily used commuter lines it was however deemed uneconomic. The line's main passenger traffic was workers travelling from the Wigan area to industrial plants in Cadishead/Partington and around the docks in Salford and Manchester. Until the late 1970s the Lancashire United bus company operated a replacement daily bus service from Wigan to Partington. On the original site now stands the Grand Arcade Shopping Centre which was built between 2006 and 2008.

Above: Pupils from the Notre Dame School for girls turned out on Worsley Terrace, Wigan, to see King George V and Queen Mary. Taken during the 1913 royal visit.

Below: This photograph will bring back many memories to Wigan girls who attended Notre Dame School for Girls in Standishgate. Judging by the motor car in shot and the length of skirt, this picture probably dates from the late 60s or early

70s. Mary Quant began experimenting with shorter skirts in the late 50s and this culminated in the creation of the miniskirt in 1965, named after her favourite make of car, the Mini. To gain this effect on school skirts the more rebellious girls used to roll the waistband over and over to achieve the desired length. There is a record of the convent of Notre Dame in 1854, with a college for pupil teachers and a High School for girls. In the background is the spire of St John's church which was a good refuge for pupils during cold and wet playtimes. The school closed in 1974.

endowment. What happened in 1597 was that the School was endowed and it has continued from that day without a break. The school pictured is actually the fourth building, opened on 11 October, 1937, by the Rt. Hon. Oliver Stanley, President of the Board of Trade. This school was built on the same site as the previous school which was demolished to make way for the new building. The picture is taken from Parson's Walk, in front of what is now the Wigan School for the Arts building. To the right is tree lined Mesnes Park Terrace. The Wigan Grammar School building is currently home of the Thomas Linacre Centre, part of the NHS.

Above right and below: The history of Wigan Grammar School dates from 1597 and possibly earlier, although any previous school was not permanent, because it had no regular income or

LOCAL HOSTELRIES
Around the pubs of yesteryear

reigned supreme in their establishments and stood no nonsense from their mainly male customers. Selling Burton ales, the hostelry was still popular later in the last century with students and shoppers alike. Commercial Yard connected Market Street with Market Place, but its buildings were demolished to make way for the Marketgate Shopping Centre.

Top right: To an outsider, Wigan Lane sounds as if it is a little country road, meandering sweetly through a few Lancashire hamlets. Locals know better as it is part of the A49 that runs north of town towards the M6 and Preston. Even in 1900, The Beehive was well placed to enjoy quite a lot of custom from the passing trade. It was owned by the Burton Brewery and enjoyed a fine reputation. However, these delightful children would never take a drink inside as the pub closed its doors in 1907, leaving them to look elsewhere to slake their thirsts.

Right: The demon drink was classified as one of the main causes of family strife in Victorian and Edwardian times. In fact, Lloyd George would later describe alcohol as one of the nation's biggest enemies during the First World War because it disrupted the production of munitions and military equipment vital to the war effort. Even before then, it was quite common to see groups of men sitting around idly, just waiting for the pub to open. A number of men are seen here waiting for the Douglas Tavern to open in Chapel Lane. To a man they are wearing a bowler hat, which was the fashion of the time. The Bowler hat, also known as a coke hat was originally created in 1849 for the British soldier and politician Edward Coke, the younger brother of the 2nd Earl of Leicester. The bowler hat was popular with the working class during the Victorian Era. During the Silent Film Era, Charlie Chaplin's character "The Tramp" almost always wore a bowler.

Remember when pubs were places at the end of the street or in the town centre where you could get a peaceful pint? On a Saturday night, you could go down there, sit in the lounge bar and enjoy a night out with the missus. She might sip a port and lemon or gin and orange, but it did not matter which. The waiter always knew his customers and, for a tip of the odd tanner, kept the drinks coming at the merest of nods. On other nights we went into the tap room for a game of darts or crib with our pals. Let us go back to some of those old haunts.

Above: It was not unusual to see women running pubs and beerhouses even before Mrs Pankhurst and her supporters had won the vote for the fairer sex. Those such as the landlady of the Commercial Hotel, in Commercial Yard, did not worry too much about equality. They were beyond and above all that as they

Above: The Eagle and Child took its name from the legend of the man who wanted a male heir to carry on the family name. As his wife was of advancing years, it seemed unlikely that this would ever happen. One day, when out walking, they found a baby boy close to an eagle's eyrie. The bird had presumably stolen the infant and carried it away. The couple rescued the child and brought him up as their own son. The legend has other origins and twists, depending upon where you are in Europe. It also might rely on how many times your glass had been filled and then emptied during an evening spent here, telling tall tales.

Below: The Alexandra Hotel, on Whelley still stands opposite Canon Sharples School, though it does not look like the pub in this photograph any more. It used to be a Magee and Marshall's house, selling fine India Pale Ale, among its other brews. The brewery was founded in Bolton in the 1860s by David Magee and took over Marshall's in 1885. The company also swallowed up the Wigan Brewery on King Street and became one of Lancashire's best known brands. Today, it tends to be Stella Artois rather than IPA at the Alexandra.

Left: The Big Lamp Hotel at 7 Wallgate was sandwiched between two others, the Golden Lion to the right and the Raven to the left. Seen in c1880, conversation in the public bar might well have mirrored the talk we hear today. The war in Afghanistan would have been on many people's minds. There were several campaigns in that part of the world during the Victorian era. At the time of this photograph, some 40,000 British troops were fighting out there with mixed success. Perhaps some lessons are never learned. The Big Lamp was taken over by the Golden Lion, but it closed in 1969.

Below: Market Place was well known, perhaps even notorious, in Victorian times for the number of pubs, inns and alehouses it supported. By 1869, there were 10 in this small area, with the White Lion Hotel being one of the best patronised. In later years it advertised the sale of 'Family port and magassar oil for footballers' bruises'. The oil was better known as a hair restorative, so we can only presume that soccer players were a bit like Ernie Wise with short, fat hairy legs! The owners of the White Lion also made sure that drinkers kept up to date with Wigan Athletic's progress as it had a telegraph link to the ground so that half time and full time scores could be supplied.

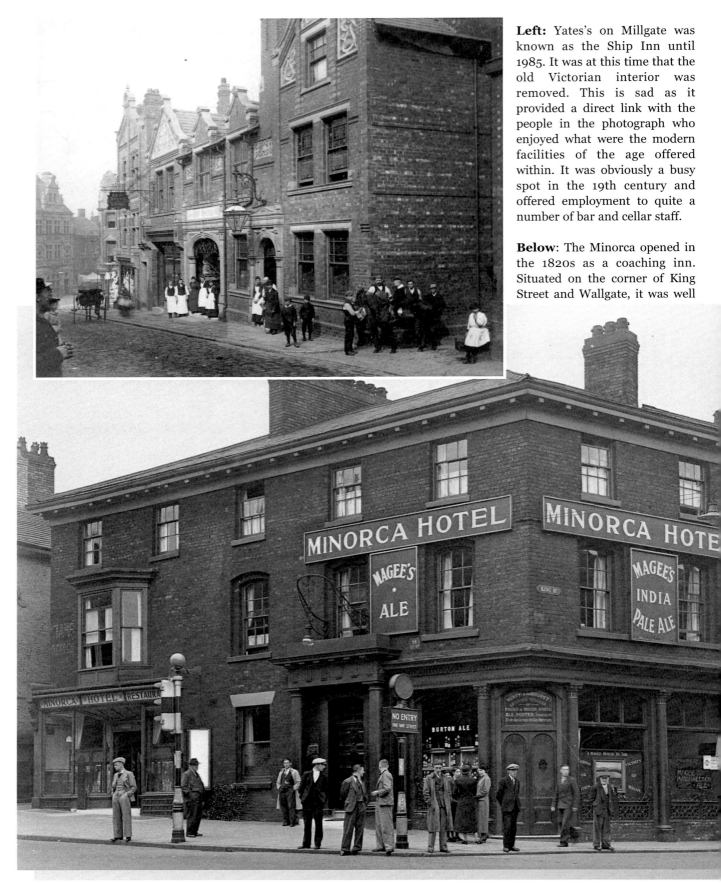

Left: Yates's on Millgate was known as the Ship Inn until 1985. It was at this time that the old Victorian interior was removed. This is sad as it provided a direct link with the people in the photograph who enjoyed what were the modern facilities of the age offered within. It was obviously a busy spot in the 19th century and offered employment to quite a number of bar and cellar staff.

Below: The Minorca opened in the 1820s as a coaching inn. Situated on the corner of King Street and Wallgate, it was well

them to play with. He never did. In fact, he always had something a bit sweet on his breath and a silly grin on his face when he returned from his evening out. It was only later that the kids twigged to the fact that he was in the Skelmersdale Arms. Situated at the top of High Street, it enjoyed both a local and a passing trade.

Below: The Old Dog Inn, on Market Place, was up for sale in 1970. Its day was done as one of the empire created by Peter Walker, of Warrington. The company owned many of the pubs in Wigan. Although merged with Tetley in 1960, it still kept its own name on its houses as it had a proud and historic pedigree of brewing beer. Founded in 1864, it expanded in the early 1900s by the acquisition of many smaller enterprises, including Oldfield's, the Albion Brewery and Airey's.

placed to catch the overnight trade of the traveller who needed to break his long distance journey. The hotel targeted the top end of the commercial spectrum for its clientele and soon established a healthy reputation for fine ale and good food. Formerly a Robinson's house, along with many others in the vicinity, it came under the ownership of Magee and Marshall in 1894. This brewery underwent a period of rapid expansion around the turn of that century as it took over a number of smaller enterprises. It also made particular investment in inns and hotels at seaside resorts, notably Blackpool and Southport. Magee's, as it was generally known, was taken over by Greenall and Whitley, of Warrington, in 1958. The Minorca later became known as Berkeley Square and then The Berkeley.

Above: High Street runs through 'Skem', as locals refer to their town, from the Marie Curie roundabout to the old Liverpool road to the west. Going to see a man about a dog meant nothing of the sort, though it did fool quite a few children who thought that dad was bringing back a pooch for

EVENTS & OCCASIONS

Below: It is funny how many Britons suddenly become Royalists when there is a party, celebration or festival to be enjoyed. There is quite a number who sit around muttering about the expense of supporting a monarchy and the poor example set by some of its dependants, but come the day of the special occasion, out they pop. They leave their armchairs and emerge onto the streets and pavements, literally flying the flag. It was just the same over 100 years ago. Queen Victoria died in 1901 and, the following year, the Prince of Wales was crowned as King Edward VII. He was a well known philanderer who was the opposite of his staid mother. Despite the reservations some had for his style of kingship, everyone united behind the throne. Britain still lived up to the 'Great' part of its name as the map of the

world was still coloured red in many places. It was also the dawning of a new century and an age that promised much in technology development. So, we festooned King Street and the other main parts of town with supportive messages, banners and jolly bunting. The coronation took place on 9 August 1902 in Westminster Abbey.

Right: The 15th Lancashire Fire Engine Rally took place in Market Square. This was a collection of the finest examples of fire fighting resources and manpower that could be assembled in 1890. The sight of such high tech equipment attracted a large crowd to witness the scene. In Victorian England, fire was a dreaded, regular occurrence. Homes and businesses were often crammed close together and it only

industrialised and mechanised, sparks created by moving parts often ignited waste materials with devastating effect. A co-ordinated response from trained personnel using dedicated equipment was needed. Many of the early brigades were funded by insurance companies anxious to protect themselves from large claims, not all of which were honestly made. Gradually, local councils and authorities acknowledged their responsibilities and formed their own fire services.

Below: A bakery on New Street, Pemberton was the scene for this snapshot, of life in 1926. Although one or two smiled for the camera, most turned a pained and anxious face towards the racks of bread in front of them. This was a handout point during the General Strike when the impoverished relied on charity for the basics. Typical of the British, there was no pushing and shoving as everyone waited his turn. It was a period of great austerity and hardship, as witnessed by the drawn faces that so many of those queuing displayed. Just a few years earlier, Lloyd George had spoken on behalf of the government he led at the end of the Great War and promised working people 'homes fit for heroes'. He forgot to mention that they would have insufficient funds and not enough work to make them affordable.

took a few moments for fire to take hold and sweep through a mill, warehouse or block of terraced housing. Relying on people passing buckets of water along a chain was obviously ineffective. As factories became more

Above: The parade of boys and young men took place in the first decade of the last century. Interested bystanders looked on as the throng made its way along Church Street, in Upholland. The men in the centre of the road appeared to be acting like some sort of trail bosses on a cattle drive across the American prairies. You can almost imagine Frankie Laine singing 'Rawhide' as an accompaniment. The children were turned out quite beautifully. Mums had scrubbed those little faces so that they shone bright pink, despite the protestations of those in receipt of such treatment. Although they dare not say so, the majority of these lads would have been far happier playing in the streets instead of marching along them. Upholland still holds a regular form of walking day at its annual pageant when local churches and schools combine in a parade that includes festive floats and marching bands.

Top right: Carrying posies of flowers and decked out in the whitest of white dresses, these girls proudly walked down the street in an outward sign of their Catholic beliefs. They were members of the Sacred Heart parish in c1930 and what an honour it was for the one chosen to lead the parade or carry the church banner. Usually held on Whit Monday, this annual display was never one to be missed. Of course, thanks to the vagaries of the English climate, we could not guarantee the sunshine each and every year. Yet, even though we had to battle through the elements on occasion, we did so with heads held high. Sometimes our shoes pinched a little and the dye from the banners and streamers ran on our soaked dresses, but we accepted it as a price worth paying.

Right: Wigan Market was a seething mass of humanity as the world and his wife attempted to make some sense out of what appeared to be little better than a rugby scrum. The noise of both humans and animals was deafening as each tried to outdo the other. The smells were also something else, with a mixture

of odours coming from both bodies and dung with a force that made the strongest of stomachs jib just a little. Somehow, goods were traded and sold on. Stalls and barrows were set up and baskets laid out. Purchases were made and taken back home. Pickpockets, of course, had a field day and the taverns and inns around the square did a roaring trade. The lord of the manor first held a market in the town in 1258, and look what he started.

The Market, Wigan

Right and below: The Wigan Carnival was first conceived way back in 1926 by a group of church dignitaries who had the foresight to see it would be an excellent way to raise much needed funds. In the following years each Carnival would have a main theme which was of interest and relevant to the area. The Carnival procession made its way through the town each year and it could extend back for several miles. The procession made

Green Lane, in Ashton-in-Makerfield. The news of the accident came as a sad blow for there had not been a serious accident at the colliery for almost thirty years. Tragically, 27 miners lost their lives underground on that fateful day.

its way to Market Square where it was judged and the prizes handed out. They then proceeded to Bull Hey cricket ground for the festivities, where there were stalls, bands, dancing and an amusement fair. These pictures are from the 1929 Carnival with 'Wigan on Wheels through the 20th Century' as the theme.

Right: A thought provoking and emotive picture, believed to be Gerard Street, Ashton in Makerfield, in 1932. It shows the funeral procession for men killed by an explosion on 12 November, 1932, at Edge Green Colliery, The Colliery was situated off Edge

Above: Wigan's war memorial was designed by Giles Gilbert Scott and unveiled in 1925. Funded through public donations, the monument is now a Grade II* listed building and commemorates the fallen soldiers from the town in the First World War and other conflicts. In 2006, the plaques bearing the names of the dead were stolen; a year later they were replaced through council funding. This is a picture from that day, as hundreds of local people stand with pride and watch Sir Herbert Lawrence dedicate the war memorial outside the parish church.

Above and right: The Lancashire and Yorkshire Railway (L&YR) opened the line between Liverpool and Lostock Junction (west of Bolton on the Manchester to Preston line) on 20 November 1848. The original L&YR station at Wigan was located east of the current station, closer to the London & North Western Railway (L&NWR) station.

The early train services on the line ran to Liverpool, Bolton, Bury and Manchester. The railway opened between Wigan and Southport in April 1855. Wigan's L&YR station was then relocated to a position west of where Wallgate station is today. In 1896 Wigan finally received a railway station in line with the town's size and importance. In 1978 the Victorian-era buildings on the station platform at Wallgate were demolished and new structures erected. The street level building remained largely unscathed.

Below: That's one way of keeping your feet dry. Wallgate Bridge under a foot of water was blocked to most forms of wheeled traffic when this photograph was taken in the 1930s. This area of Wigan was susceptible to flooding for many years, the cause being the nearby River Douglas which frequently spilled over its shallow banks, much to the inconvenience of local people. The bridge itself had a very distinctive advertisement for the Victoria Hotel which, according to the sign, offered 'first class accommodation and catering'. The Victoria Hotel, in Wigan, was established next to Wallgate railway station in 1894, two years before the station itself was opened.

This page: Happier thoughts spring to mind when looking at the picture above for it features the steps of St. Paul's Cathedral in London, on the day of the Coronation of Her Majesty Queen Elizabeth II, in 1953. It was a tremendous honour for Wigan Boys' Club Band to be asked to play here, and their efforts were certainly appreciated by the thronging masses who were waiting to catch a glimpse of Her Majesty. London had been dogged by grey clouds on the day. The Coronation was the first opportunity that the country had to hold a mass celebration after the war, and it is nice to see Wigan's contribution on the celebrations in the Capital in this lovely photograph. The second picture proudly shows the band at a special reception at the Granada Cinema, Kensington, London on 24 October, 1953. The band are introduced to the Mayor and Mayoress of Lambeth.

Right: At first glance you might think that this was an outing put on by the Co-operative Society. But, you would be wrong as there is no hyphen in the name. The train headed for Blackpool had been chartered for the day by the management of Coop's Mill, on Dorning Street. This happy group of trippers looked forward to a day of fresh air and fun, strolling along the front or visiting Blackpool Zoo and keeping a careful eye out for the lion that ate Albert, if you believed the old monologue. The clothing factory was built for Timothy Coop in 1871 and extended from four to six storeys in 1888. It is now a listed building.

Below: Quite why the youngster is riding away from the tables that are groaning with goodies is not recorded, but perhaps he had been sent to get someone who was missing. Surely, he would not have turned his back on this 'do' for any other reason. As a nation we do love our street parties. In modern times holding one is perhaps the only time that people from one end of the street meet those from the other. When we were young or our parents were growing up, then neighbours were known as 'aunty' or 'uncle'. Even though we were not related to them, it felt as though we were because we felt close to them. There was a better sense of community. When VE Day was celebrated in 1945 or the Coronation in 1953, then it was a straightforward job for mums to don their pinnies, have a quick chat with other ladies nearby and put on a spread fit for a special occasion.

Above: The streamers and bunting are decidedly home made. In fact, some of it has the look of something that the rag and bone man rejected, but the children did not mind. They were enjoying their very own Maytime street party. Elsewhere, other groups had grand pageants and put on an expensive show with garlanded floats and grand costumes, but who needs such frippery? These kiddies were just as happy with their own May Queen who could be feted just as royally around the table that had been covered with a makeshift cloth upon which tasty jellies and iced buns and fairy cakes could be found. Most of them put on something special. The girls found party frocks and some of the lads came along as pirates or waving a cap pistol as they pretended to be Jesse James or Wyatt Earp.

Below: Silcock Brothers' fair has come to town, by nightfall it will be in full swing. Even in October 1963, Freddie Cannon and Eddie Cochran were still being played over the loudspeakers, some time after their careers had peaked. 'Palisades Park' and 'C'mon Everybody' were hit records from a few years earlier, but they were just the right sort of songs to

get people in the mood for the big wheel, dodgems, waltzers and merry-go-rounds that we enjoyed so much. When night fell, teenagers went along and shared sticky toffee apple kisses and candy flossed cuddles behind the hoop-la stall. Groups of giggling girls cast glances at dark haired Romeos who manned the sideshows and were just the sort of young men that mum had warned them about. Goodness, some of them wore tattoos on their arms and the odd one had an earring! Whatever next? The funfair was sometimes referred to as the 'pot fair' as it had once been associated with the sale of kitchenware and other household goods. The backdrop was taken up by the Civic Buildings on the far side of Market Square that were once the base for Oates and George Rushton's grocery business. The building dates from 1905 and was a symbol of Rushtons' success in developing a chain of 60 shops across the area in the last century.

Top and above: It may be breezy and it might rain soon, but we are going to enjoy this street party come hell or high water. That was the message being sent out. It looks as if everyone else on Bank Street was staying put, but this doughty group had spent an age stringing the bunting across the road and buttering the bread. With party hats and mock crowns firmly in place, it was time to pay homage to our Queen. On 7 June 1977, Platt Bridge echoed the sentiments of the whole nation as it celebrated the Silver Jubilee. Although February marked the month in 1952 when Elizabeth became our monarch, a week in early June was set aside for the celebrations in the hope that the sun would shine.

Right: This was the largest and grandest of shopping experiences that you could imagine. To Victorian eyes, this was the equivalent of a hypermarket on any large out of town retail park. Yet, here it was, in the centre of our hometown. Wigan Market Hall opened on 21 May 1877, having cost a mammoth £40,000 to build. A marvel of modern engineering, it was a mass of metal girders and crossbeams, with some ornately cast trappings to add that touch of class. As the town's first covered market, it did away with the old stalls that had been a nuisance for

horse drawn traffic to negotiate as the carts and carriages tried to cross Market Square. When the Galleries opened in the mid 1980s, the old Market Hall was incorporated into the development scheme and sited at the corner of the clock tower that was designed to imitate the campanile in Venice's St Mark's Square.

Left: Makinson Arcade can provide a link with one of the most famous of Britain's high street stores. In 1891, Michael Marks came to Wigan, having had some success as a trader in Leeds with his penny bazaars. He established a distribution centre on Great George Street, near the railway, before joining forces with Thomas Spencer in 1894 and opening stalls in the Market Hall and Makinson Arcade as a forerunner to our town's first Marks & Spencer store on Standishgate. The decorations we see here were put up in honour of King George V who was due to visit Wigan during a tour of the northwest in 1913. The taking of the photograph probably had something to do with James Millard who had a photographic business in the arcade. His son,

AROUND THE SHOPS

William, is the man in a short sleeved shirt, standing in the doorway to the left.

Below: It is probably just a few years after the last war when the photographer made this visit to Market Place. Women were out and about in coats and dresses that had hemlines that were mid calf in length. During the early 1940s, clothing rations meant that there was nowhere near enough material around to be used on long, flowing styles. Its just after noon as shoppers take a look in the windows of the shops along Market Place. The shops in this row include, Watersworths fruit shop, Hunters and Bakers Jewel Casket (advertised as 'the shop you can trust for quality'). The shop was acquired by Goldsmiths in the mid 80s and has undergone significant sympathetic restoration. Further along from Baker's is Bolton's the well known local ironmongers. In 1998 the refurbisnment of Market Place was completed and was subsequently chosen as one of the best new public spaces across the country, by a leading group of design experts. The highly praised central mosaic, designed by sculptor Sebastian Boyesen, commemorates the granting of Wigan's charter by Henry III in 1246.

Above: Motor buses had replaced the trams, even though the tracks of the latter could still be seen in this view of Market Place in pre-war days. The tower of All Saints, our parish church, cast its shadow over the buildings below. Parts of it are medieval in style, reflecting its 13th century origins. The perpendicular Gothic style was part of the remodelling that occurred some 200 years later. The adjoining Walmersley Chapel dates from 1620. Shoppers enjoyed the privileges of moving from one individual store to another, rather than having to make their way into a purpose built mall that is just like any other centre in any other town. Wigan folk have been luckier than most, in that respect, as big is not necessarily beautiful. We should breathe a word of thanks that, unlike many other town centres we could mention, you know where you are when you visit Wigan.

Top right: Victoria House was the home of the popular department store owned and operated by Lowe's. This photograph, thought to date from the late 1950s, shows the front of the store from the direction of Market Place. Many, perhaps more mature Wiganers will have fond memories of the cafe, located upstairs in the store; it was a popular meeting place, and widely regarded as the place to be and be seen in by local people. The demolition of the building was considered to be a sad occasion by Wigan shoppers,

though there was one silver lining for townsfolk which should not go unmentioned; for as long as people could remember it had been impossible to get a view of the Parish Church from a reasonable distance, simply as a result of the proximity of the surrounding buildings. During the time that Victoria House had been cleared, and before the modern building which replaced it had been constructed, local people could view and photograph the church in a new light.

Right: Many changes have taken place in this part of town since this photograph was taken the year after the end of the war, in August 1946. The picture is beautifully composed, with the familiar clock tower of the Parish Church peeping over the rooftops. Many of the retailers shown will be familiar to more mature readers; Lee's Cafe, Fletchers and the Olde Dog Hotel on the left hand side of the picture. In the centre of the picture we can see Victoria House, the location of the much-loved department store known as Lowe's. Note the lovely ornate lamp standards which blend so well with the tudor-style buildings in the photograph. The atmosphere is completed by the nostalgic effect brought about by the double decker bus, the stern-faced lorry and the curvaceous motorcar in the picture. Pure nostalgia!

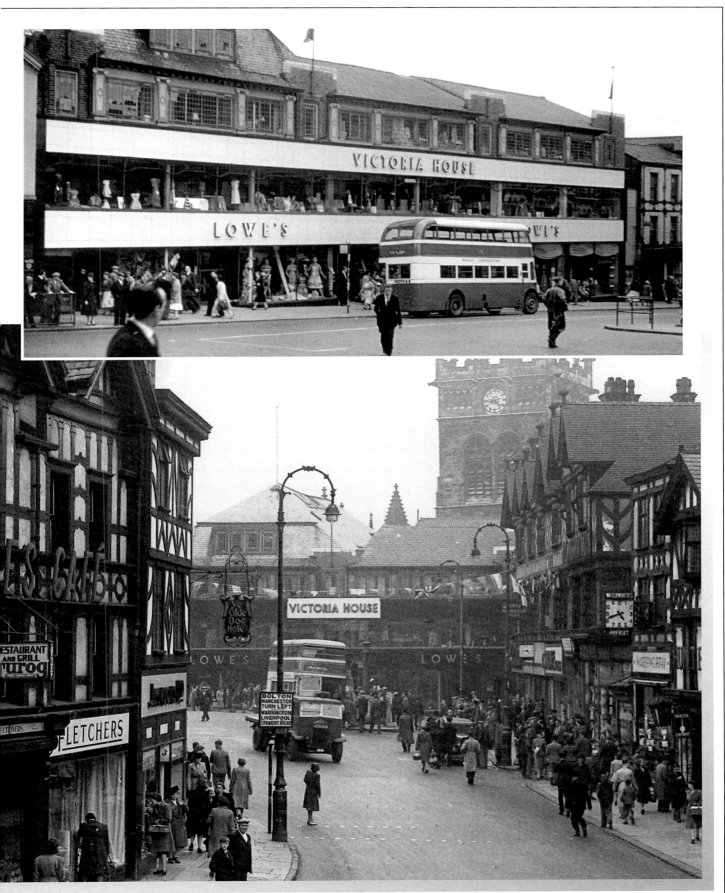

Above: This picture reveals just how much the act of shopping has changed over the years. It is over sixty years old and has an almost museum-like appearance. There are tell-tale clues as to the ethos which underpinned 1930s retailing practices; most obviously the presence of a chair - a minor point but evidence that shopkeepers in the 1930s were not simply interested in taking your money and getting you out of the door. In those days it seems that people had more time for each other, and that personal service meant just that. Another clue to the era featured here include the immaculate glass barriers along the front of the counter to prevent eager little hands touching the merchandise - and the shiny metal weighing scales which would have been put to frequent use.

Right: The crowds were out in force on a bright and cheerful day as the 1950s drew to a close and the swinging 1960s dawned. All of a sudden, Britain realised what Harold Macmillan had said about 'never

having it so good' was actually true. Gone was the austerity and drabness of postwar times and we looked forward to more profitable and prosperous times. Like the 1961 pools winner, Viv Nicholson, it was spend, spend, spend. Across Market Place, at the junction of Millgate and Standishgate, the timbered-style building belonged to Woolworth's store. Later, it would do service as Menzies newsagents before passing into the hands of WH Smith. The shopping areas of The Galleries and the Marketgate Centre have changed the picture completely in many places down at ground level. Fortunately, some of the upper reaches of the shops have kept their period look. Even the new centres have tried to hang onto the Tudor style by using the bargeboard and gable shapes of the buildings they replaced. The large number of buses reminds us that car ownership, though on the up, was still not universal. Arms full of bags, many a Saturday shopper struggled through the crowds and onto public transport for that journey home.

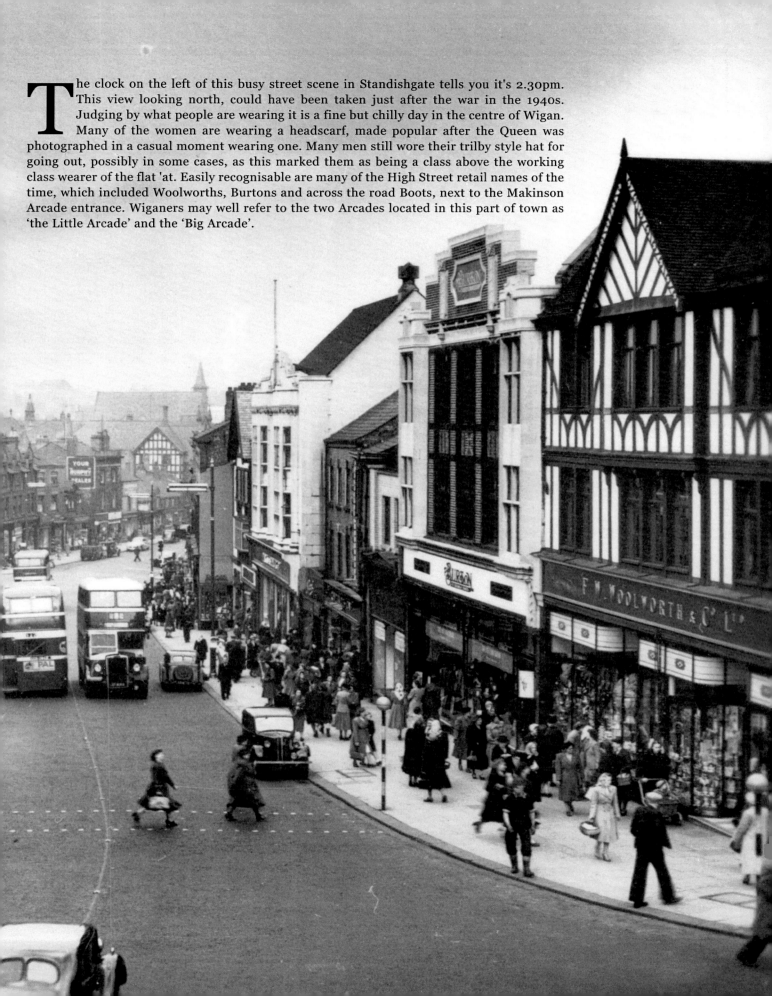

The clock on the left of this busy street scene in Standishgate tells you it's 2.30pm. This view looking north, could have been taken just after the war in the 1940s. Judging by what people are wearing it is a fine but chilly day in the centre of Wigan. Many of the women are wearing a headscarf, made popular after the Queen was photographed in a casual moment wearing one. Many men still wore their trilby style hat for going out, possibly in some cases, as this marked them as being a class above the working class wearer of the flat 'at. Easily recognisable are many of the High Street retail names of the time, which included Woolworths, Burtons and across the road Boots, next to the Makinson Arcade entrance. Wiganers may well refer to the two Arcades located in this part of town as 'the Little Arcade' and the 'Big Arcade'.

Above: Before there were supermarkets, big grocery shops had assistants to fetch your goods for you off the shelves behind. Photographed in the 1950s we can see Marjorie Dodd and Jean Sutch behind the counter at William Latimer's grocery and general provisions store in Market Street, Hindley. The store was next door to the Britannic Assurance Company and close to the Post Office. The actual experience of shopping for groceries was very different in the 1940s and early 1950s than it is today, there were no supermarkets so all the shopping had to be done at various shops in the high street. You went to the butchers for your meat, the greengrocers for your fruit and veg, the fishmongers for your fish and so on, there was no one place where you could get all of these products. This was to change as the very first American type

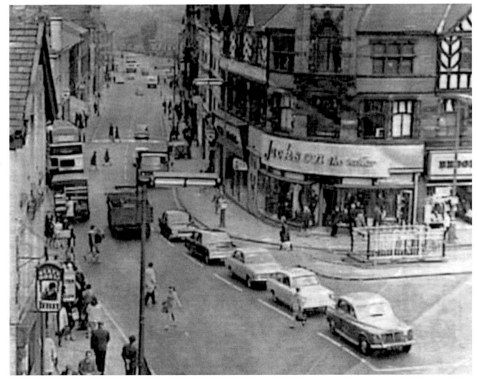

'serve yourself' stores were starting to make an impact in the 50s.For the first time shoppers experienced something that we now all take for granted, walking around a store helping themselves to the goods then taking them to the checkout. Such a mundane and ordinary part of living today. For Majorie and Jean however, it was business as usual, providing the people of Hindley with an essential sevice and a friendly smile.

Bottom left: It is shoppers who now wait for one another at the Market Street corner of Market Place. Seen here on the corner, Jackson the Tailor, was one of the most famous menswear brands of the sixties and seventies. At its peak, Jackson the Tailor had more than 550 shops across the length and breadth of the UK and was seen as the place to go for a suit for special occasions such as weddings, job interviews and first dates. It even was mentioned in a script for TV show The Likely Lads. But the firm went into administration in 1978. The front of the queue of cars is the Rover P4, the mainstay of Rover during the 1950s and through to the early 1960s. In the middle of the 19th century,

the town centre was surrounded by tightly packed courts and cramped two and three roomed cottages. Sanitation was poor and living conditions generally dreadful. Just a single lifetime on and this was the picture. Wigan was now a clean, smart place to be.

Below: Looking down Standishgate from Market Place in the late 1950s, the traffic coming towards us is an indicator of the rise in fortunes of the ordinary Briton at that time. The last ration books and coupons were put away in 1954 and we started to move towards a more prosperous and generally more cheerful time. Car ownership, once the preserve of the middle classes, became something to which the working classes could aspire. Before long, it was not just an ambition, but a reality. Affordable saloons, such as the Ford Popular and Prefect, the Morris Minor and the Mini, put us on four wheels instead of two feet. The young woman on the left, just stepping onto the zebra crossing, had probably just left Makinson Arcade, behind her. This was built in 1897, the year of Victoria's Diamond Jubilee.

TRANSPORT

Below: For a while, it seemed as if steam would be the answer to providing more local public transport than the railways could offer. It looked as if this was the logical progression. After all, coal fired locomotives had revolutionised cross country journeys, so why should they not do the same in and around our towns? Wigan flirted with horse drawn trams as an alternative, in addition to steam powered ones like this example pictured at the Market Street-Bridge Street terminus in Hindley. The section of tramway from Wigan town centre to here opened in 1883. The driver and conductor posed on the steam loco section that was attached to the passenger trailer car. This was quite a modern looking affair as many early tramcars had open tops. The cars were built by William Wilkinson and Company, a local Swinley firm that patented a superheated steam process in 1881.

Above: This could be a scene from a yard on Sodor, the fictional island where Thomas the Tank Engine and his friends are based. The reality is a little more mundane as we are looking at Springs Branch that was part of the London and North Western Railway. It was here that the Manchester and Wigan Railway was connected to the Northern Union Railway in the early 1890s. Any steam train enthusiast would drool at the sight of this line-up in real life. Even those of us who have outgrown the pastime can still recall the excitement of going down to a station platform, bridge or level crossing, armed with an exercise book, pencil, Thermos and a packet of sandwiches. A whole day could be spent quite happily writing down engine numbers and munching away merrily. We were careful with the cup of tea in case it was knocked over and spoiled our day's work.

Above right: Registration marks with two letters at the beginning were first issued in 1903. As this car would seem to have just a two digit identifier following the letters 'EK' it is safe to assume that it was registered in that early part of the 1900s. EK denoted that the car was registered in the Warrington district that also included Wigan for such purposes. Therefore, we are looking, in all probability, at a local family. It must have been one that had plenty of cash

behind it as motoring was something that the well-to-do practised in Edwardian times. This handsome machine offered an exhilarating ride as well as a draughty one. Mum, dad and the children squashed up behind the chauffeur with the best seat being given over to the dog.

Right: This was as sleek and as chic as public transport delivered by Wigan Corporation Tramways (WCT) could get. The car could just about be called streamlined. But for the fashion styles of the men on board, the reader would be hard pushed to deny that this machine hailed from the final quarter of the last century rather than the first. The straightening of the roads and the demolition

of the clusters of small buildings close to the town centre around 1900 made movement so much easier. Lampposts doubled up as carriers for many of the cables, in addition to those standards that were purpose-built. WCT was formed in 1880 when steam and horse were used as power sources. Electrification arrived around the turn of the century and, at its peak, there were 25 miles of tramway leading out from Market Place.

Left: The tramlines were still there, but only in use in certain parts of town. Electric trams were on the way out and would finally disappear from Wigan's streets in 1931. Trolleybuses were the obvious answer until diesel engined motorbuses took over completely. They were able to use the overhead cabling system that powered the trams, so the cost of replacing them was minimised. This trio from the Corporation fleet was busy on Parson's Walk, alongside Mesnes Park to the right, in 1925. Just a single car, further back down the boulevard, adds to the certainty that we relied heavily on public transport to get around. People who grew up in that era wondered how their parents and grandparents managed before electricity came to our streets. Youngsters asked, 'You don't mean you had to walk?' when discussing days gone by; so some conversations have a familiar ring to those of today.

Above: We can presume that this was Market Street, Atherton, in the early 1940s. The front bus has blackout stripes painted on its front. The blackout began in Britain on 1 September, 1939, two days before war was declared on Germany. Everyone had to cover windows and doors at night with heavy curtains, thick cardboard or even paint. If a chink of light showed, then a warden would let rip with what became a traditional 'Put that light out' bellow. It is unlikely that a Junkers pilot at 20,000 feet would have seen anything, but that is how it was. Streetlights were switched off or dimmed extensively by the use of hoods. Kerbs and lampposts were painted with stripes to help people find their way. Cars had to use the faintest of lights. Not surprisingly, the number of people hurt and killed on our roads rose alarmingly, despite petrol being rationed and journeys limited.

Below: This lovely old photograph records a hive of activity on Market Square, with charabancs lined up to take their excited passengers away to the coast. Whether the occasion was an annual Wakes holiday, or a Bank holiday is uncertain. After the war their was a steady increase in the popularity and, for most people, the affordability of holidays and day trips, and thousands of working people would take advantage of the economical, locally-organised trips to get some well earned rest and relaxation. Facing Market Square, the red brick building known as the 'gas showrooms' can be seen, and to the right, the old bus station and the buildings beside it which have now been demolished. The sea of cobbles which formed the the Market Square have, sadly, long gone; they found use as much more than a market area over the many years they laid here, and are now covered by the Galleries Shopping Centre

Left: Hope Street Congregational Chapel overlooked Market Square and the old bus station. This place of worship was built in the 1880s, replacing a former chapel on the site. It was demolished in the early 1970s, giving way to Barclays Bank. That just about summed up the changing attitudes in Britain in the last quarter of the 20th century. Money became the new religion as prophet turned into profit. The bus station was an integral part of the town centre as we relied heavily on it before we were all able to afford motor cars. It was also somewhere that couples finished off their Saturday night date. If you went out with someone who lived in Standish and your home was in Garswood, then saying your goodbyes at the bus station made sense. It was an awfully long walk if you took her home on the last bus.

Below: Wigan has been a 'market town' since the 13th century. Little is known of the presence of an indoor market before 1875 when preparations began to erect a new market hall. It was completed in 1877 at a total cost of £40,000 and officially opened on 21 May of that year. Situated on Market Street, it soon became a busy thriving place. The market hall enjoyed much popularity until it was demolished in 1988, bringing to an end over a century of Wigan's history. It was replaced by modern galleries and a shopping complex. The former Market Hall was honoured by a Royal Visit, when King George V and Queen Mary arrived on 10 July, 1913.

Above: The unusual chassis on this Wigan Corporation Tramways Leyland double decker makes it stand out as it tuns the corner into Standishgate. It seems strange to those of us who presumed that Woolworth's would go on for ever to regard this view as historical. Since the five and ten cent store, or threepence and sixpence shop in English, came to our shores from America, it became a fixture on every town's main shopping street. Between the two world wars, each town seemed to add a Burton, Marks & Spencer and a Woolworth to its shopping experiences. They became fixtures that we thought would never vanish. Woolworth's, with its pick 'n' mix, cheap fragrances, dodgy bath cubes and poor man's recordings of other people's hit songs, sold its stuff at knock down prices. The jewellery was more plastic than gemstone, but we all knew that. But, in the first decade of the 21st century, it disappeared and became just another statistic.

Right: If ever you had heard Justin Timberlake sing then you might well want to swap him for a car, but this bus passing under the bridge at the bottom of Scholes was from an era 20 years before this former boy band singer was spawned. The JP registration mark firmly identifies the number plate as being from Wigan because local traffic usually carried JP, EK or ED in its lettering. The Horseshoe pub was the last watering hole before leaving Millgate on the way out of town. Situated close to the corner with Station Road, it led the way to a large number of beerhouses that a drinker could happily find along the road to the old Scholes village. By the way, Timberlake's was a garage on Wallgate.

The Austin A30 was being filled up at Diggle's Garage on Warrington Road, Goose Green. An attendant, or Billy Diggle himself, looked after us, filling her up as well as checking the oil and water. He even said, 'Thanks', when we paid him our five bob. This was in the early 1960s before self-service took over everywhere, especially shops and garages. The trend now even includes some restaurants and canteens and, in a way, our banks as we get our cash from a hole in the wall.

Below: 'Keep going well, keep going Shell'. This was just one of the slogans that petrol companies adopted in an effort to encourage the motorist to use their products. 'Put a tiger in your tank' was Esso's response.

Above: Originally called Blague Gate the station was renamed as Skelmersdale in August 1874. The station was situated on the Ormskirk to Rainford Junction line, together with a second line which ran from Rainford Junction to St Helens. Following a post-war years decline in passenger numbers this culminated in the closure of this line in 1951. The Skelmersdale line which provided trains between Ormskirk and Rainford Junction, continued for passengers until 1956.

Left Hindley is one of the main stations on the Wigan to Manchester line. At the time of this 1956 view of a steam locomotive waiting at a deserted platform, it was known as Hindley North, differentiating it from Hindley South. The latter closed in 1964, in the middle of the Beeching era of swingeing cuts. However, for a place of modest size to have supported a pair of stations shows how popular and important rail travel once was. There were also others not too far away at Platt Bridge and Hindley Green, though these both closed in 1961. Just two platforms remain in use here today, with only overgrown evidence remaining of two others for fast lines that were decommissioned in 1965.

Above: Train spotters have to be quick on the uptake these days. Blink and one has whistled past before they realise it. So often, a train contains but a small handful of carriages. In the golden age of steam, sturdy and handsome locomotives happily pulled a line of carriages that ran into double figures. They were filled with passengers as well. This one was southbound, hauled by an ex LMS 4-6-2 Princess Class locomotive, designed by William Stanier and built in Crewe in the mid 1930s. It remained operational until the early 1960s. This example was passing through Boars Head Junction, Standish, on the West Coast Line above Wigan. The signal box that closed in the early 1970s had to be straightened up at one time as it leant precariously over the line as a result of mining subsidence.

WORKING LIFE

Right: Skelmersdale UDC had its very own fire brigade at the turn into the 20th century. It may not have been a rapid response unit, but the officers in charge of the appliance did their best. Here they posed proudly with their sturdy horses beautifully groomed, awaiting the moment when the scene would be captured for posterity. The men's helmets glinted in the sunlight and looked most impressive. They were the sort issued to most firemen, but were soon discarded and replaced. They were found to be good conductors of electricity and a fireman's hair soon stood on end when his headwear came into contact with a live wire during an incident. The dangers of a watery mix with electric cables and metal objects were only then fully appreciated. Skelmersdale lost its individual fire service as the town declined in influence and size, but regained the use of its own station in 1965 on the site of an old egg packing plant. A new station was built on Tanhouse Lane in 1971.

Below: If you are going to learn to drink sensibly and responsibly, then start off young. Even so, this little chap was probably just too wee to be introduced to the charms of cask ale. Two and threequarters is pushing it a bit. Possibly this was the landlord of the Railway Hotel at Appley Bridge in 1921 and the other men with him were definitely draymen. The clothing worn by those featured even marks out the worker from the semi-

manager. It was very much the case in class conscious Britain that social strata were clearly defined. Here we have flat caps and aprons versus a waistcoat and watch chain. The hotel used to have stables and offer overnight accommodation. Being close to the canal, it could offer service to the men and beasts with the horse drawn barges.

Right: The caption on the picture suggests extra payment as someone needs another bump on the window to rouse him from his slumbers. It seems amusing and almost beyond belief that someone was actually employed to get people out of bed in the morning, but the knocker-up man performed an important role. Armed with a clock and a list of who needed wakening and when, he patrolled the streets on behalf of both the employer and employee. No work, no pay, so it was worthwhile for the latter to be sure of getting to the mill on time. Even being a minute or two late meant an hour's pay off the wages for the day. Two questions can be posed from this image. First, can we borrow this chap and turn him loose on our teenage son upstairs and, second, who knocks up the knocker-upper?

Below: You did not get long for your lunch in Platt Bridge. E Manghall's family run fish and chip shop recognised this and was only open for a single hour from midday at lunchtime. Working hours were long, so there was no sense in reopening at what we now call teatime, so Mr Manghall waited until 8pm before popping his Grimsby fish into its batter and cutting up his potatoes using a hand cranked chipper. Who had the simple but brilliant idea to marry fish & chips together is the subject of fierce controvercy and we will probably never know for sure. Some credit a northern

entrepreneur called John Lees. As early as 1863, it is believed he was selling fish and chips out of a wooden hut at Mossley market. For generations, fish and chips have been eaten with greasy fingers, out of paper, on a seaside holiday, a pay-day treat at the end of the working week or a late-night supper on the way home from the pub. So important were they during World War II, ministers bent over backwards to make sure fish and chips were one of the few foods that were never rationed. Even George Orwell in The Road to Wigan Pier (1937), put fish and chips first among the home comforts that helped keep the masses happy and "averted revolution".

Below and right: You have to be of a certain age to recall seeing a bobby on a bike or using a roadside telephone. The line of officers was spotted in 1930 at Wigan Cricket Club. The officer on the left of the Cycling Contingent is thought to be Cliff Hamilton. He was a member of a force that was respected and trusted to carry out its duties responsibly and fairly. Children listened to what their local policeman had to say and never called him 'plod', 'pig' or something worse. If they did, then it was a clip round the ear and another one to follow from dad if he got to hear about the cheek. The force was also a good subject for popular songs. 'If you want to know the time, ask a policeman' was a music hall favourite

and Charles Jolly's 'The Laughing Policeman' from the 1920s was still being played by Uncle Mac on 'Children's Favourites' in the 1960s. The telephone used by PC Lowe in 1957 helped him contact Police HQ. Before personal radios were in everyday use, it was a problem keeping in touch. These telephone stations were positioned at various points along a busy beat and had a light on top that would flash to alert a man on patrol that he had to contact his station. There was also a handset provided for public use to give someone a hotline to the centre in case of an emergency.

Right: Arthur Robins and Ernest Waite ran their furniture business

from Penson Street, a small road that runs east off Wigan Lane. There is no evidence of the enterprise there now, with just a community youth centre on this street, The Swinley bar and club backing onto it and a mortgage broker on the corner. The firm of cabinetmakers was one that offered a form of professional workmanship and expertise that is not easy to find anymore. The company could turn its hand to restoring antiques and creating reproductions, as well as creating something modern. In 1930, serving an apprenticeship while learning a trade demanded dedication and aptitude. Becoming a time-served craftsman did not come easily.

As the industrial revolution took hold, Britain witnessed a transformation in its economy and its population in the way in which it earned its living. Rural communities gave up the land and moved to small towns, swelling the number of inhabitants so that they became larger centres of population and even cities in their own right. The expansion of overseas trade and the technological changes that helped mechanise home based industry altered the face of the country. Remarkable inventions changed how we worked and, especially in the north of England, the traditional cottage industries of spinning and weaving became major mechanised ventures. Water mills and then steam driven machines led to an integration of processes. Initially, large mill buildings were multi-storey affairs, demanding large windows to provide as much daylight as possible. These were complemented by single storey weaving sheds. Early Victorian mills were clustered around canals that provided both water and a transport network, but could later take account of the building of rail access to help in the movement of raw materials and finished goods. The workforce was almost exclusively female. As with these Wigan mill girls in their weaving sheds and spinning mills, they worked with heavy, noisy machinery. It was hot and dangerous work. Until banned by laws, children were used to crawl under looms and spinning frames into confined spaces to help free blockages or collect waste fibres. The belts and moving parts on the looms sometimes came loose or were hurled across the shed when a piece malfunctioned. Crushed bones and maimed limbs were all-too-frequently occurrences. Yet, despite being deafened and having lungs clogged and damaged by cotton fibres, the women often spoke fondly of their time with mules, flying shuttles and jennies and could converse easily with talk of weft, warp and the Jacquard loom. They remembered best the friends they made. It was those who made the work worthwhile.

This page: Part of the style of clothing worn by pit brow girls can be linked with the Coal Mines Act of 1842 that banned women from working underground in the mining industry. This was unpopular with these female workers as it deprived them of their livelihood and, with the collusion of mine managers and owners, many dressed as men and carried on working just as before. Gradually, the practice ceased and the pit brow lasses, as they were generally known in Lancashire, got jobs above ground. These included pushing wagons to the stock heap, stacking coal and raking it through for stones. They continued to wear rather masculine attire that gave them a distinctive look. This scandalised Victorians as they put on trousers with the legs partly rolled up underneath hardwearing skirts. Their heads and hair were protected from the coal dust by thick headscarves. They were as tough as the old boots that they wore, as you can tell from the stances adopted by the lasses from the Junction Pit photographed (top) in the early 1900s. The pit was located off Bickershaw Lane, near the Queen's Hotel. The larger group of girls, seen in May 1949, worked at the Maypole Colliery, in Abram. Even then, people still discussed the terrible disaster of 1908 that put the Maypole on the front pages when an explosion killed 76 workers. The women at the pithead continued to resist attempts to stop them from working and the lasses were still employed in such work until the last ones were made redundant in 1972 at the Harrington No 10 Colliery, Lowca, in Cumberland.

Kathleen Silcock, Patricia Wade. Eat your heart out Miss World.

Below: "Putting you through now caller". The girls on the switchboard of Wigan Telephone Exchange were up to date with 1920s' technology, under the watchful gaze of their supervisors. This was decades before direct dialling came in. Back then, you spoke from your own phone or one in the street to an operator who made the connection on your behalf. In more rural spots, you could have a cosy chat with her, but not here. Efficiency was the watchword.

Top: We made some great friends at Eckersley's Mills. They were the sort of girls you could share a joke with, but even more you could share a secret. If there was a problem at home with a husband or boyfriend, then a bit of homespun advice from the pal at the loom alongside was worth its weight in gold. Eckersley's had six spinning mills and was well known for its Cat's Head Yarn.

Above: Showing a very glamorous leg or fourteen, this bevy of beauties acted as guides at the HJ Heinz Factory in 1969. Visitors to the Kitt Green site were provided with the most attractive of escorts that you could ever wish for. It is not surprising that some red blooded males found a reason to make a second or third visit whether or not they had any real need to do so. Left to right: Judith Rainford, Ann Mason, Rosaline Prescott, Maureen Prescott, Janet Golding,

R Banks & Son - The Final Service

The loss of a loved one is always a difficult time. Thankfully the profession of funeral director has evolved, not only to help organise funerals but also to provide a plethora of sound advice in such troubling days.

In the early decades of the 20th century after the doctor had certified death, one usually called the 'Layer Out'. Every village and street once had such a woman.

'Last Offices' were carried out by those stalwart ladies who attended to all a family's deaths - and births. The undertaker was summoned to take the necessary measurements and details. Having made the arrangements with the family, a date and time would be fixed for the funeral to take place. The undertaker would then arrange for his men to make the coffin.

The firm was established in the 1920s. With its Head Office now at Halliwell House, Ormskirk Road, Pemberton, the firm has five branches: Hallbank House, Wigan Road, Bryn; Clifford House, Grove Lane, Standish; Windsor House, Scholes, Wigan, Whitley House, Gidlow Lane, Beechill, and Parsonage House, Railway Road, Leigh.

R. Banks & Son has come a long way since it was founded in 1921 by Richard Banks. Until then Richard had been a taxi driver but, helped by his son Herbert, he combined the role of taxi driver with that of undertaker. The combination of taxi services and undertaking was not in itself unusual - though the Banks' headed notepaper of the 1940s 'R Banks Funeral Director - Weddings a Speciality' looks a little incongruous today.

Clifford Halliwell joined the business in the early 1960s as a part-time driver and funeral assistant. Herbert Banks asked Cliff if he would consider taking the job on a full-time basis. Cliff agreed, and over the next few years gradually took on the role of funeral director himself.

Herbert Banks eventually became ill and his doctors told him it might be a good idea to sell the business as the stresses and strains of the job could easily worsen his deteriorating health. Cliff Halliwell now bought the business and slowly developed

Top: Founder, Mr Richard Banks. **Left:** Richard Banks (right) and his son Herbert Banks . **Below:** Herbert Banks and Harry Worthington pictured awaiting the bride and groom outside St Matthew's Church, Highfield.

Once the coffin had been constructed the undertaker and his men would then deliver it to the house. In many cases, the doorways were too narrow to take the coffin so windows had to be removed by the undertaker's carpenter and replaced after the coffin had been taken in. The front room or parlour of the deceased's home would have been chosen as the last resting place until the funeral. It was not until the late 1950s that Chapels of Rest began to be widely provided by undertakers.

Today, a local family-run business, R. Banks & Son (Funerals) Ltd, is one of the largest independent funeral directors in the area; it offers all the wide range of services expected of the profession today.

what was then a very small enterprise into a significantly larger family business.

In 1974 Cliff's son Brian joined him, bringing new ideas of his own. Instead of traditional old limousines modern stretched vehicles were introduced. The business developed steadily, and in 1982 a new funeral home and head office was built in the centre of Pemberton and named Halliwell House. In the late 1980s the first branch was opened at Bryn Cross, Ashton in Makerfield. The early 1990s saw a second branch opened at Windsor House in Scholes.

In 1996, like Herbert Banks before him, Cliff Halliwell himself retired due to ill health. His son Brian became Managing Director, helped by his mother, Cliff's wife Elsie. Sadly, Cliff Halliwell passed away on 28 September, 1998. His funeral was attended by hundreds of people from all over the United Kingdom. The service was held at St Matthew's Church, Highfield, Wigan, where the Reverend Bill Harrington, the vicar of St Matthew's, officiated at the service assisted by a dear friend of Cliff's, Rector John Southern, who was vicar of St John's Pemberton - the parish which the firm had served over so many years.

In 2000 a third branch was opened at Grove Lane, Standish, and named Clifford House in memory of Cliff Halliwell.

Richard Edwards, Managing Director of Edwards Funeral Directors, based in Dicconson Terrace, Wigan, approached Brian Halliwell in 2002 to enquire if R Banks & Son Ltd was interested in buying the Edwards business. In November 2002, R Banks & Son Ltd acquired the Edwards business, with Richard Edwards continuing as manager.

Yet another expansion project would come to fruition in 2004 when the former funeral home of John Monks & Son, respected funeral directors in Leigh, was acquired. Extensive alterations and upgrading were carried out. The premises in Railway Road were renamed Parsonage House after the local colliery which had once employed so many people in the Leigh area.

*Top left: Mr Clifford Halliwell(left) and Mr Herbert Banks. **Above:** Delivery of the new Ford fleet in 1984, from left to right Clifford Halliwell, Brian Halliwell and Andrew Naylor of Woodall Nicholson coachbuilders. **Below:** Members of staff outside Charnock Richard crematorium with horse drawn hearse.*

The 1999 Daimler had has been modified into a hearse by Wilcox and Co of Chalfont St Peter. Brian adds: "It was bought from a funeral car trader who had got it from Leverton's of Euston in London, the royal funeral director. But it was only when we got it and found pictures and documents showing that it had been used after the funeral service on 5 April, 2002. The Queen Mother's coffin had been carried on a gun carriage, but was transferred to the hearse for the final part of

Only full time staff are employed at R Banks & Son: the same people take care of all funeral needs, from start to finish. Every funeral is as individual as the person who has died, and all services are tailored to the specific needs and wishes of the family.

Those services include the conveyance of the deceased to one of the firm's private chapels of rest. A wide selection of coffins and caskets is available. When it comes to choosing a memorial as a dignified tribute to a loved one the firm's brochure contains a large range of memorials and headstones. Given the firm's early heritage it will come as no surprise that clients can choose from a variety of vehicles. But Wigan folk about to make their last journey can bring a regal touch to their funerals.

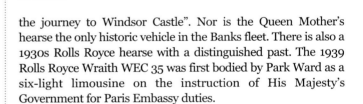

In 2009 Brian Halliwell discovered that the hearse he had just bought was the one used in 2002 to take the late Queen Mother to her final resting place. It was only when Brian opened the glove compartment of the newly delivered Daimler that he discovered photographs and documents proving its illustrious history. Since then there has been quite a demand for that specific vehicle. According to Brian "I was taken completely by surprise by this historical connection. We are always looking to update our fleet and bought both a new limousine and the hearse. We paid £30,000 for the hearse. It is a beautiful vehicle."

the journey to Windsor Castle". Nor is the Queen Mother's hearse the only historic vehicle in the Banks fleet. There is also a 1930s Rolls Royce hearse with a distinguished past. The 1939 Rolls Royce Wraith WEC 35 was first bodied by Park Ward as a six-light limousine on the instruction of His Majesty's Government for Paris Embassy duties.

Top left: A military funeral held at Wigan Parish Church. *Above:* Funeral of Rugby League legend Terry Newton with John Close DipFD walking in front of the hearse at the D.W stadium. *Below left:* Managing Director Brian Halliwell pictured alongside the hearse, now part of the Banks fleet, that carried the Queen Mother to her final resting place. *Below:* Brian Halliwell pictured with Neville Bullock, former bodyguard to Winston Churchill and the 1939 Rolls Royce Silver Wraith hearse .

Prime Minister Neville Chamberlain used the Wraith during his ill-starred peace negotiations between France and Germany. Newsreel of the time captured Chamberlain travelling in the limo.

Before the fall of France WEC 35 returned to London and, following a change of Prime Minister, Winston Churchill was photographed leaving 10 Downing Street in the vehicle. After the war, on 1 January, 1946, the Rolls Royce returned to Paris to resume its role at the British Embassy there.

Jennifer Halliwell MBIE runs the personnel side of the business and is also company secretary. Brian and Jennifer's son and daughter, Martin and Carina, have also joined the firm.

For almost a century the name of Banks has been associated with funerals. Today the Halliwell family ensures that the Banks name retains its long-held reputation for dignity and excellence.

Following its disposal in 1953 WEC 35 was rebodied as a hearse by coachbuilders Alpe & Saunders, of Royal Kew Gardens. The vehicle was re-registered on 7 August, 1953, with a new number plate NYM 267. It has now been fully restored.

The Banks & Son family firm is a member of the

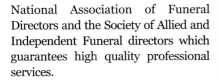

National Association of Funeral Directors and the Society of Allied and Independent Funeral directors which guarantees high quality professional services.

Today, the company is still run by Brian Halliwell MBIE DipFD; his mother Elsie is now retired. Brian's wife

*Top left: Brian Halliwell, Carina Halliwell and Catherine Heaton present a cheque for £6000 to the Rainbow Ward at Wigan Infirmary raised at the company's Summer Ball charity fund raiser. **Top right:** Brian Halliwell (back row third left) pictured with the Aspull Football team who are sponsored by the firm. **Left and above:** Brian Halliwell with Wigan Warriors Thomas Leuluai at the D.W stadium when R Banks sponsored the rugby match. Above are members of staff and guests at corporate hospitality. **Below:** R Banks & Son's Ormskirk Road, Pemberton, headquarters.*

Edwards Funeral Directors
Reliability, Efficiency and Dignity

One of the most difficult times for any family is dealing with the passing of a loved one. Happily the profession of funeral director has evolved to help with much of the burden.

Edwards Funeral Directors, along with their predecessors, members of the Wood family, have been privileged to serve the community of Wigan for well over a century. The firm takes great pride in its independence and the highly personal, affordable service its staff offer to all their clients.

The current firm of Edwards Funeral Directors was started in 1993 by Richard and Susan Edwards. Both had been qualified funeral directors for many years, and had worked for Middleton & Wood, the local firm that was previously run by Susan's father, George Wood,

and by his father and grandfather before him. Under Susan's forbears, and her husband's leadership as Managing Director, Middleton & Wood had, over the course of more than a hundred years, become one of the pre-eminent firms of funeral directors in the UK, having built what was generally regarded within the profession as the finest funeral home in England - Egerton House.

Susan trained for two years in London under the watchful eye of John Kenyon (the only funeral director who would take a female trainee at the time!). She gained her Diploma in 1969 whereupon she returned to Wigan to take an active role with Middleton & Wood for the next 14 years.

After George Wood died in 1974 Richard Edwards was asked by the shareholders to take over as Chairman and Managing

*Above: Susan and Richard Edwards. **Left:** 1930s Middleton & Wood wedding cars. **Below:** An early Middleton & Wood horse drawn carriage.*

Director. The following nine years, up to 1983, saw the business grow dramatically by the acquisition of other funeral directors in Orrell, St. Helens, Ormskirk and Southport, as well as by adding a number of local branches within the Wigan area. The high standard of personal service that had always been paramount at Middleton & Wood was infused into the acquisitions with major capital investment in buildings, vehicles and staff training.

Unfortunately, in 1983 a large public company made an offer to the 30 or so shareholders. The majority were inclined to accept and the company was sold, a move which was not welcomed by some of the active Board members. After a number of years, during which ownership changed several times, Richard left and, with Susan, started Edwards Funeral Directors in 1993 at Holmwood, Dicconson Terrace, a beautiful building a couple of hundred yards from Wigan town centre. The building which had formerly been Barker's Restaurant was tastefully modified to provide a modern, yet homely, funeral home.

Speaking at the time of the reason for starting up again in the profession at the age of 47, Richard said: "When you and your family have been directly responsible for 100 years in setting standards of service through a particular business it is not unnatural to want to place your talents at the disposal of the public, particularly in your own home town."

Edwards Funeral Directors quickly established for itself a reputation for providing a highly personal service with reliability, efficiency and dignity.

Making provisions for your own funeral is probably the most thoughtful decision you could make. Increasingly, people are considering funeral arrangements in advance, for peace of mind for themselves and their family.

The business was one of the first to offer Pre-Paid Funeral Plans in association with Golden Charter, the nation's largest provider to the independent sector with currently over £300m held in independently administered trust funds.

The firm now receives many enquiries about its 'Golden Charter' and 'Help the Aged' prepaid funeral plans.

Health problems, however, meant that Susan had to retire early. Soon afterwards it was decided that the future of the firm would be best secured by joining in partnership with the leading independent Funeral Director in the town, R. Banks & Son., who had come to the fore once Middleton & Wood had come under corporate management.

The partnership extended with the R. Banks' network so that it now has six local branches in the Wigan area, as well as representation in Leigh, the eastern half of the Borough, all of which offer the personal service that only an independent Funeral Director can provide in a family's hour of need.

Top left: A 1930s hearse. *Top right:* Two funerals directed by the firm down the years.

Tim Calderbank Metal Recycling

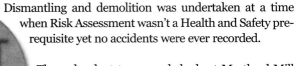

Elias Calderbank was born on Primrose Day, 1875, in Great George Street, Wigan. He began his scrap metal business in 1904, originally working on the railways whilst his wife, Elizabeth, ran a bake house they owned in Platt Lane, Scholes. When customers couldn't afford to pay for their bread they would accept scrap metal in payment. This began their trade in metal but on leaving the railways Elias had to return until he had raised enough capital to pursue his love of the scrap metal business.

The original depot was a small yard behind the current Wigan Little Theatre. Here they hired out pony and carts to local rag and bone men, buying their collections at the end of the day. The business grew steadily, and as soon as their children were able they all joined the business. There was Joseph, John, Thomas and Elizabeth. The company was incorporated in April 1924 and began trading as E. Calderbank & Sons Ltd.

The Calderbank family were proud of their motto 'Spot Cash' and each employee was supplied with a brass badge with the motto engraved. The phrase is still used today even though many customers prefer digital banking and electronic payments.

With the arrival of their first lorry in the Twenties, Calderbank's last working horse, 'Teddy', was retired to a local farm in Chorley Road, Standish, only to escape and be found waiting the following morning outside the Wigan yard gates ready for work!

Dismantling and demolition was undertaken at a time when Risk Assessment wasn't a Health and Safety pre-requisite yet no accidents were ever recorded.

The redundant trams and sheds at Martland Mill were demolished in 1926 and in November 1929 the legendary Wigan Pier was bought from Winstanley Collieries for £34 and dismantled for scrap.

By the mid 1930s Calderbanks had a fleet of motorised vehicles and over twenty men engaged in collecting scrap. At the outset of the Second World War half of the vehicles were

commandeered for the war effort but the company still prospered as scrap metal was urgently sought. Railings were removed from public buildings and even Wigan Parks

*Top: The brass 'Spot Cash' badge each employee was supplied with. **Above left:** 'Teddy' ready for a days work. **Below left:** World War One tank dismantled from Mesnes Park. **Above:** Removal of the original Wigan Pier. **Below:** A World War One gun.*

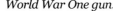

ornamental gates were sent for scrap. Luckily for Wigan, Calderbanks were reluctant to cut them up, and returned them to the Council when the war ended.

The company began managing many works contracts and larger premises were sought. In 1938, a nearby mill came up for sale which was across the River Douglas from the famous Central Park rugby ground. This was known as Water Heyes Mill, Orchard Street. Later, a further site was purchased that included

Today, the business is highly mechanised with mobile shears and balers. Prices are at record levels and the volume of material destined for China has increased significantly.

Tim Calderbank Metal Recycling is now based on an award-winning environmental site at Bradley Hall, Standish, which has also seen many changes over the years. During the Second World War it was a large munitions factory, then in 1948, H.J. Heinz opened it as a food manufacturing plant.

Tim Calderbank has personally served over 100,000 customers. However, he is still waiting to see if Lloyd and Liam the fifth generation of Calderbanks, will continue the family tradition.

Top left: Old gas lamps arriving at Orchard Street yard. Top right: Woodhouse Lane tram depot. Left: Large electric motors being loaded. Below: An aerial view of the company's award-winning Bradley Hall site.

a rail link at Britannia Bridge, Ince. Rail passengers travelling from Manchester to Wigan always knew they were approaching Wallgate Station as they passed the heaps of metal piled high.

The next generation of family now joined the firm; there was John's son Joe, and Tom's two sons Frank and Elias who continued to build up the business until they all retired in 1987.

Thirteen years earlier, Frank's second son, Tim, had formed his own metal recycling company in nearby Standish. His elder brother Andrew joined a few years later, followed by younger brother Matthew, who had been working at E. Calderbanks, then sister Jackie. Matthew later left and trained to become an airline captain. Tim's wife Janet joined the company in 2007.

A&P Cole Car Sales Ltd - Wigan's Biggest

A & P Cole is Wigan's biggest independent used car dealer. The firm, with three used car centres in Wigan, Wrightington and Whelley, sells a wide range of quality used cars.

The firm now has one of the largest selections of cars in the area, with over 240 vehicles typically on offer.

Before the start of their car sales business, however, Alan and Pat Cole worked in totally different jobs. After their marriage in 1975 Alan took a job as a milkman.

The hours suited their needs. Alan worked from 5am till 11 am. This enabled him to work on cars in the garage at the rear of their house. Pat was a part time evening cleaner. They both worked hard, saving up with the intention of starting their own business. Originally it was to be just a workshop repairing cars. Then one day they came across an advert to rent at the side of a petrol station at Bolton Road, Ashton in Makerfield, on the outskirts of Wigan.

That was the start of A & P Cole Car Sales. On 1 June, 1982, their £5,000 savings allowed them to buy a caravan to convert into an office, £700 for the first rental instalment, and £3,500 to purchase five cars.

Pat's father, Bill, sold the first car within a few days. Bill was always there to help when needed.

The Coles stayed at Bolton Road for 12 months, unfortunately the garage was due to be sold so they had to look for other premises.

Alan and Pat moved onto temporary sites until in 1983 they asked a local garage owner in Wrightington if they could rent part of his forecourt. He agreed and before long Alan and Pat were established and the business began to flourish. Alan's role was to buy the cars, both he and Pat valeted the cars, Pat sold them and completed the accounts and Alan serviced them before customers took delivery. And their unique guarantee started.

Alan and Pat offered customers their own guarantee. They thought this to be a more personal touch than a Mechanical Breakdown Warranty. Customers could speak to them directly should they need to, and all guarantee work could be carried out at their convenience. It proved to be very popular.

Top: Founders Alan and Pat Cole. **Left:** In the early days. The company's converted caravan offices in Wrightington. **Above:** The company's Miry Lane premises.

Soon A&P Cole were able to employ a full time motor mechanic. This helped the firm grow. And Pat could fit her working hours around daughter Jackie who was by now at junior school.
In 1984 A&P Cole managed to purchase the rented land at Wrightington and built a car showroom there.

The business continued to grow. In 1996 another site was found in Eaves Lane, Chorley which had a large forecourt and car showroom. Daughter Jackie now joined the business.

Within a few years, however, the Eaves Lane site was sold when another site at Miry Lane, Wigan, was bought. The site was in a poor state and required a lot of adapting: the Coles did a lot themselves to keep the costs down.

Jackie Cole married her husband Andrew Glover in 1997. In 2002 Andrew joined the business and A&P Cole purchased its third site, in Whelley, Wigan. This again required huge renovation. The business was now incorporated as A & P Cole Car Sales Limited. The directors are Alan, Pat, Jackie and Andrew.

Andrew is involved in vehicle preparation and after sales and works alongside the Sales Manager Barry Schofield. Many of the 21 staff have been with the company for many years. Garry Clayton used to attend the same school as Alan and Pat. Bill Jackson has also been with company for many years, a respected member of the sales team. Jeff Roe is the Manager of the Whelley branch alongside Andy Vose, Manager at the Wrightington site.

Motor mechanic Darren Kavanagh was one of the first on the payroll; he is now based at the Whelley garage. Tony West has been with the company for many years based at Miry Lane. Kayne Fillingham and Lee Mather, valeters based at Miry Lane, have also worked for the company since the early days.

Meanwhile the A & P Cole family has now grown, with two grandchildren Jack and Sammy. Another generation of car salesmen in waiting!

*Top left: A & P Cole's Dangerous Corner, Wrightington, site. **Above left:** Pat's father Bill who was always there if needed. **Above:** Pat Cole pictured after completing the Flora London Marathon, 2009, raising £3,000 for Diabetes UK. **Below:** The A&P Cole Whelley, Wigan, site.*

Belmont Packaging Ltd - Packaging Solutions Provider

Boxing Clever - Pioneer to 21st Century Manufacturer

The ubiquitous cardboard box is something familiar to us all. Corrugated paper was invented in England in 1856, and first used as a liner for tall hats. Corrugated cardboard was patented and first used as a packaging material in 1871. The patent was issued to Albert Jones of New York City for single-sided corrugated board. Jones used the corrugated cardboard for wrapping bottles and glass lanterns.

Scottish-born Robert Gair invented the pre-cut corrugated cardboard box in the 1870s. Gair's invention came about as a result of an accident: he was a New York printer and paper-bag maker; one day, whilst he was printing an order of seed bags, a metal ruler normally used to crease bags shifted in position and cut them. Gair discovered that by cutting and creasing in one operation he could make prefabricated paperboard boxes.

In recent times the role of cardboard packaging has evolved into more than just a device for transporting and protecting goods as they move from one place to the next.

Today corrugated packaging is used everywhere, from postal packaging to the trays holding products on supermarket shelves, right up to major displays in cinema foyers.

In over 30 years of business, and based in Hindley Green, Wigan, Belmont Packaging Limited has been at the forefront of this evolution in the use of corrugated materials. In the process it has become one of the most capable packaging manufacturing plants in the UK. Over 50 million units per year are produced to meet the demands of a wide variety of national clients, ranging from major blue chip companies to small 'cottage industry' users who buy relatively small quantities via the internet.

From its beginnings in the summer of 1978 Belmont thought differently than its competitors. The business was one of the very first 'Sheet Plants' in the country (a corrugated product manufacturer who buys in 'sheets' of cardboard and converts relatively small volumes to serve niche markets).

Above: *Belmont's first order, received on 18th July, 1978.*
Below: *Early "Team Photo"; Mike Moloney, far right, with his team outside the original factory in Lowton, Leigh, 1983.*

Despite the tough economic conditions of the time, and a weakening manufacturing base across Britain, building commenced in 1984 of a single 20,000 sq ft factory with single office block ready to house a dozen machines and what was by now nearly 20 staff, including those who made the transition from Leigh.

Company founder Mike Moloney had a vision to supply the market in a very particular kind of way in that pioneering era.

In the back room of a house in Bolton, overlooking Belmont Village, perched on the side of Winter Hill, Belmont Packaging Ltd was born.

Belmont's first order was received on 18th July 1978. With an interested market and the support of the first suppliers and

Working closely with the niche markets that Mike Moloney had identified at the company's inception, and following further investment, the 'sheet plant' business continued to prosper. The firm invested continuously in pursuit of its goal of creating an efficient, well-equipped, skilled and profitable business.

In the mid 1980s Belmont Corrugated, Belmont Engineering and Belmont Transport were added to the core business activities, with Belmont Corrugated beginning its life in Worsley, commencing trading there whilst a second 20,000 sq ft factory was built in 1986 to house the early 'Thistle' corrugators back at the main Wigan site.

With the corrugators now in place, and complementing the converting machines, output grew further. Later Belmont added its own purpose built Corrugator – the 'Belmont 1100' to replace the 3 small corrugators, the machine – still a key part of today's business – is unique in the world and was the last corrugator built in the UK.

Top left: The new build Sheet Plant, Hindley Green Wigan, 1985. Left: Belmonts first export to Munster, Germany, in February,1991. Below: One of the first: Investors in People presentation in June, 1992.

customers, the first premises were acquired in Lowton on the outskirts of Leigh, along with the basic machinery and equipment to begin small-scale production and supply. Within a few years turnover had grown significantly, as had the small team of production and office staff working closely with Mike to ensure the company's ambitions and vision were achieved.

With infrastructure, machinery, capability and skills coming together the company soon outgrew the Lowton plant and decided to make the leap to a new, green-field site in Hindley Green on the outskirts of Wigan.

A high bay, fully racked warehouse facility was added later, capable of holding over 400 racked pallets in support of customers' requirements in the supply chain.

With a well-organised, highly skilled team in place, and an asset-investment strategy second to none in the sector, Belmont continued to gain a reputation for good business, high capability levels and integrity. Its trade-supply arm grew rapidly; competitors saw the market but lacked the capability and investment to match Belmont.

Belmont now became one of the foremost suppliers to the Trade (its own competitors). These developments, and good business practice, did not go unnoticed, with Belmont securing the North West 'Business of the Year' Award in 1997; testimony to the hard work and vision of its people.

Belmont now cemented its place as a main player in the Sheet Plant sector of the corrugated industry. The company made its first export deliveries to Ireland, Germany and France, and continued to find new markets for corrugated as the world began to move more and more towards recyclable materials for transit and display solutions.

The firm's expansion was rapid, underpinned by a strong belief in its people and skills. Belmont was one of the first companies in the country to secure 'Investors In People' accreditation, via its philosophy of staff shared-responsibility, input and reward. Early principles the company continues to follow to this day.

The 1990's saw more investment and growth into specialised new markets such as high quality print and multipoint gluing. Belmont was one of the first to anticipate the retailing trade's move into shelf-ready packaging and display. The investment in cutting edge machinery now enabled fully printed packaging to complement Belmont's existing standard corrugated packaging manufacturing capabilities.

By the late nineties the plant was developed further with a third 25,000 sq ft premises created adjacent to the existing factories. This development was to be the bedrock for future growth and progression into the value-added markets including point of sale, fulfillment and stock and serve, as the market evolved further into 'just in time' and consignment stock supply requirements.

Into the new millennium Belmont continued to build on both its infrastructure and its abilities to ensure that its place in the market was sustained. Continuous investment in IT, design, material handling and machinery, including new automatic die-

*Top left: The third factory built to house some of the most advanced manufacturing machinery available to serve the packaging market. **Below**: Business of the Year award 1997; Mike Moloney (centre) with the successful Management team of the late 1990's, including Stephen Gleave (far right) who is still an active member of the current Management Team.*

cutters and case-makers, further added to its competitive edge and its attractiveness to an ever-growing customer base.

Today Belmont continues to make full use of its investment legacy and founding principles to explore how it can best apply its capabilities, skills and business philosophies to the market.

A new era began with the present Managing Director Sean Moloney.

Now under the leadership of Mike's son, Sean Moloney, he and his management team ensure the company continues the tradition of seeking out niche areas of manufacture and service within the corrugated sector, as well as continuing high end investment in new equipment and adopting the latest business concepts.

All staff are locally employed from in and around the Wigan area. They have a vested interest in the company via the Employee Benefit Trust scheme, a facility whereby profits are distributed into the scheme on behalf of the staff in support of their training and well-being. The scheme is also used to fund new equipment, which the company then rents back ensuring 'asset value' remains in the trust. An interesting by-product of this remarkable 'employee ownership' scheme is that it would be hard to find better maintained machines and equipment in any similar production facility.

Today, with over 50,000 sq ft of direct manufacturing facilities, 10,000 sq ft of racked warehousing and distribution areas, and 5,000 sq ft of office space, Belmont has grown into a major player in its sector. With an annual turnover in excess of £6m, over 45 staff, and with its manufacturing capability still at the core of the business, Belmont has expanded its base and now operates in markets as varied as pharmaceuticals, food, cosmetics and electronics. Close links with its main suppliers and an acute awareness of best practice in manufacturing techniques and market presence leave Belmont well placed to navigate the challenges of 21st century business, especially within manufacturing.

Belmont's products are to be seen in all the major supermarkets of the UK and abroad. It now sells direct to the general public too via the internet, with its rapidly growing e-store division Boxed-Up.co.uk. It has also established Belmont Display, Belmont Distribution and Belmont CorriPall (corrugated pallet solutions) to complement its core business.

Belmont Packaging Ltd is certainly 'Boxing Clever'.

Top: A view of one of the production plants today – 2010. *Above left:* Sean Moloney, Managing Director. *Below:* The team at Belmont.

When you deal with Belmont, you get the whole team on your side...

Sanko Gosei UK - Positive, Scientific, Love

According to Ryouma Sakamoto, the famous 19th century Samurai, and one of the fathers of modern Japan, " If you die during battle, you will die pitching forward!" They were inspiring words that Mr Kenso Kuroda had in mind when he came to Lancashire knowing the challenges that faced him in establishing the first overseas subsidiary of Sanko Gosei.

The words summarise his philosophy: that we should be positive in our work, complete tasks in a scientific way, dealing with facts, and that we should all have a dedication and passion for the business.

Skelmersdale was chosen because of its good links to motorway networks, central location and development grants. The site had been cleared in the late 1960s to make way for the development of the Skelmersdale Newtown and the Stanley Industrial Estate.

Sanko Gosei was established in Japan in the 1940s to produce thermo-moulded plastic articles. Three founder members started the organisation after the Second World War, with 'Sanko' literally meaning 'three lights' and 'Gosei' relating to the materials used. Though the company was later floated on the Japanese Stock Market the organisation retains its original family links, with one member, Mr Jun Umesaki, remaining as Chairman.

In the 1980s the company began expanding overseas. Sanko Gosei UK Ltd was started by the Managing Director Mr Kenso Kuroda in 1987, with just 14 staff. 'Kuroda-San' went on to to become the Group President, but a lasting legacy in the UK has been his 'Company Mind' slogan: 'POSITIVE – SCIENTIFIC – LOVE'.

The small village of Stormy Corner was demolished during the late 1960s to make way for the industrial area: the Sanko factory was built nearby. In 1987 the building consisted of

Above: *Mr Graham Wright, Managing Director (left) and Mr Kenso Kuroda (second right), Chairman in 1990 at the opening of the new office extension.* **Below:** *Mr R Atkins (Centre) from the Department for Trade and Industry and Mr Matsumura (right) of Sanko Gosei Ltd in 1988 at the official opening ceremony which involved a traditional 'Kagami Biraki' ceremony including the symbolic breaking open of the sake barrel.*

The company's annual turnover had reached £30 million by 2000, and up to 250 people were employed at the site.

But in June 2002, whilst struggling to keep up with increasing demand, disaster struck. The incoming goods warehouse and material stores were raised to the ground after an arson attack. Having only 1.5 days worth of material stocks on site the company was forced to pull in materials from around the world to ensure that all customers' orders were delivered on time.

three industrial units along with adjoining land that allowed for expansion.

By 1990 that expansion began with addition of a new frontage. The design was rejected three times by Mr Kuroda until the architects were able to present plans that satisfied his vision.

This gave the business term 'fire fighting' a whole new meaning. But whilst the company recovered from the physical damage, 2003/2004 saw the sudden loss within six months of both the Works Engineering Manager (Andrew Towers) and the Engineering Manager (Mark Ashcroft). This was devastating to the management team as both had been instrumental not just in the construction of the building but also the culture of the company. They were sorely missed.

The UK factory started making its first tools in 1990. Between 1988 and 1991 staff were sent to work in Japan for three months' training. Initially tool designs and materials were supplied from Japan, but as the confidence grew in the UK operation it became self sufficient.

Rapid growth saw the manufacture of tools for many moulding companies including Nissan, Honda and Toyota, which were then also establishing themselves in the UK.

Today, the business continues to supply plastic trim for the automotive industry. Future investment will be focussed on 'added value processes' allowing the company to compete in a global market supplying customers with a wide range of processes and services.

By the mid-1990s the tool-making team had grown to 35. In 1994 the company secured orders for the production of the instrument panel for the Mitsubishi Carisma to be made in the Netherlands. A new purpose-built factory was completed in 1995 for the production of these parts, with up to eight vehicles per day leaving Skelmersdale.

Top left and above: Aerial view of the factory in 2005 , the different colours of roof showing the many stages of expansion over the years. *Above:* The factory pictured in 1988. *Below:* Staff posing for photo in August, 2007, to celebrate the 20th Anniversary of the Skelmersdale operation with current Managing Director, Laurence Tabner (front).

By 1996, however, plans were afoot to transfer production of the Mitsubishi instrument panel to Europe. New contracts were now obtained for the supply of interior trim parts for the new Vauxhall Astra produced in Elsmere Port, Eisenach, Bochum and Antwerp along with similar products for the Honda Accord manufactured in Swindon.

William Edwards Bakers - Cakes fit for a Queen

Baking is an art as old as civilisation itself. Perhaps even older. Certainly the trade of baker is at least six thousand years old. No matter how deep the archeologists dig through ancient ruins they always find the remains of the ovens used by our ancestors to bake their daily bread.

Roman Britain was no exception. Roman-British bakers plied their trade from London to Lancashire and far beyond. In the middle-ages England's bakers were famed for the feasts they could conjure up for Royalty. And if the less well off had to make do with bread rather than cakes, well at least the bread was made by experts.

In late Victorian times Britain's towns and cities provided employment for thousands of small local bakers, each competing to be the best. Most of these traditional family enterprises have now gone. But not all.

After over 100 years in business the William Edwards (Bakers) Ltd, based in New Street, Platt Bridge, Wigan, together with its famed retail outlet in the new Market Hall, has the distinction of

being the only business of its kind in Wigan still managed and operated by descendants of the founding family.

The Edwards' success story, however, starts in Cornwall, before moving on to Lancashire and to the tragic circumstances which would lead to the founding of this famous family business.

At the height of the Cornish tin mining industry there were around 600 steam engines working to pump out the mines (many mines reach out under the sea and some went down to great depths). But by the late 19th century as Cornish mining was in decline due to foreign competition, many of the Cornish miners emigrated overseas to developing mining towns where their skills were in great demand. Other Cornish miners travelled only as far as Britain's coal fields where their skills were still wanted.

*Above: James Edwards, celebrating after winning an award for Currant Bread making in the 1940s. **Below**: This picture dates from 1938 and shows the Edwards Bakery staff.*

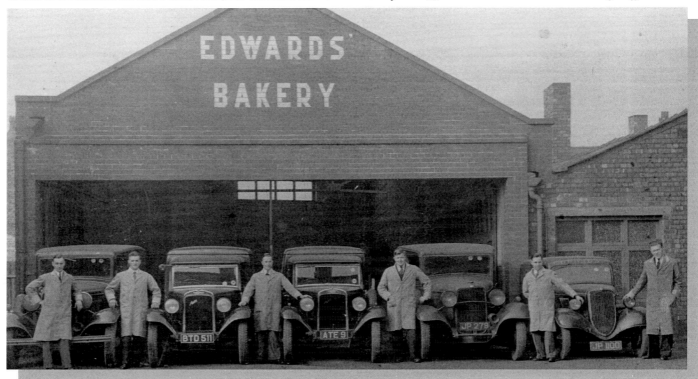

cold meats, such as its own roast ham, topside and turkey, cheeses and all the other 'goodies' required for any successful celebration.

William Edwards (Bakers) Ltd is still going strong, and still very much a family business. In recent decades many similar local family enterprises have gone, Edwards' however has survived, adjusting to changing economic circumstances and investing in modern machinery, whilst retaining its century - old traditional values.

One such Cornish mining family settled in Platt Bridge, in Wigan, finding work in the local coal pit. Sadly, the head of the household, Mr Edwards, a shaft sinker, died in 1892, leaving his widow, Anne, with a young family.

At that time there were no widows' pensions - and no welfare for miners. There was instead, however, the Poor Law, and with it the threat of the Workhouse in Frog Lane.

Even worse, the year 1893 saw a strike amongst local miners, making it impossible for the young widow to look for help amongst her equally poverty stricken neighbours.

Inspired by necessity, Anne Edwards began making pies in her little fireside oven, then she and her children went out selling them.

Anne eventually remarried to a local man called Tom Ashurst. Through William Edwards, Anne's son by her first marriage, the growing business kept the Edwards name, however.

The bakery was further developed by James Edwards in the 1930s, and 1940s, helped by his wife, Gladys. James proved to be a baker of exceptional skill and would be recognised with awards for the excellence of his products – not least his currant bread.

An Edwards' cake was chosen, in the early 1990s, for the Queen Mother's Birthday Awards in London, specially baked by Duncan, a qualified chef in the Platt Bridge Bakery. Nor was the late Queen Mother the only member of the Royal family to be associated with the from: Diana Princess of Wales visited the Edwards shop in the early 1990s.

Now well into in its second century, Edwards' Bakery continues to make oven-fresh products, not just for shops but for a variety of social functions and venues. It also supplies

The future of Edwards' Bakery is set to continue through Duncan and son of the present directors, William Edwards. The firm is famed for providing customers with quality products, not least because some of the secrets of baking excellence which began in Anne Edwards' fireside oven are still in use today.

Top left: A staff photograph from 1938. A three years old Bill Edwards can be seen on the front row, third from the left. Above: Princess Diana visiting an Edwards shop in the early 1990s. Below: Edwards' New Street premises.

Widdows Mason Solicitors - Serving the Community

Since its foundation in Leigh over 130 years ago the firm of Widdows Mason solicitors has a proud tradition of service to the local community.

Over the years, a number of long-established local firms have joined the Widdows 'legal family', including Masons of Bolton, Martin & Co. of Farnworth, Campbells of Wigan and Hindley, Linakers of Warrington and Runcorn, Burton Goodier of Runcorn and D Hampson & Co. of Shevington.

The firm now operates from six offices across the region.

The firm was established in Leigh in 1878 by Henry James Widdows. He continued in practice with his son as H J Widdows & Son until the 1930s when Eric Davis joined the firm.

In the 1940s the practice was known as Widdows, Davis & Clegg. In the 1960s it became Widdows Davis & Frankland when John Frankland became a partner. The firm became Widdows Mason in 1987 following a merger with Masons Solicitors, of Bolton.

The firm had operated from Bradshawgate Chambers in the days of H J Widdows & Son, and subsequently from a suite of offices in Turnpike House, on Market Street.

In 1996, Widdows Mason's new half a million pound head office at 18-20 King Street, Leigh, opened opposite the Bus Station. This building (formerly the 'Leigh Stores') dates from 1840 and was originally the Police Station and Magistrates' Court, being used as Leigh's Town Hall from 1875 until the present Town Hall building was completed in 1907.

The official opening of the new building was carried out by Robert Taylor, of Taylor's Confectioners, in Leigh - Widdows Mason's oldest clients.

This page: *Widdows Mason's offices: Prudential Buildings, Library Street, Wigan (top left), King Street, Leigh (left) and Hindley, Wigan.*

Campbells, with its offices at 16 Library Street, Wigan, and 10, Cross Street, Hindley, joined the Widdows family in 2001.

The Campbells firm was founded by Joseph Campbell in 1902. He practised originally from his home at 10, Cross Street, Hindley, before taking a lease on the upper floors of the newly-constructed Prudential Buildings in Library Street, Wigan in 1905.

In the 1920s, Joseph Campbell took into partnership Joseph Pasquill, and subsequently F.O. Bullough. Norman Fleming, who had started with the firm as an office boy. The practice was then known as Campbell Pasquill & Bullough.

Following the death of Mr Campbell, the firm maintained a presence at 10, Cross Street, Hindley, on a part-time basis. Only in about 1980 were the premises purchased from Joseph Campbell's descendants.

then Cyril Sykes. The firm was then known as Taylor Sons & Smith - the 'Smith' being Arthur Smith who left between the wars to become Clerk to the Justices and subsequently started the firm of Arthur Smith & Broadie-Griffith. Gerard McHugh joined the firm as a Clerk after war service and later qualified as a solicitor. When he unexpectedly died in 1977, Malcolm Capstick joined to assist Hubert Bryan Taylor who had himself become a partner in 1964.

Until Local Government re-organisation in 1974 Taylors Bridge had the distinction of being solicitors to two Local Authorities - Ashton in Makerfield, and Standish.

Following the decision of Prudential Insurance Company to vacate the ground floor of Prudential Buildings for new offices, the partners at Campbell Pasquill & Bullough bought the building, following which the ground floor was completely refurbished. In the same year, a merger took place with the firm of Taylors Bridge.

Taylors, Bridge, Baron & Sykes is believed to have been in existence since 1793. For most of its history, the firm practised from Old King's Head Chambers, at 17, Market Place, Wigan, on the upper floors of what was originally a public house.

By the middle of the 19th century the firm was known as Taylor & Sons. Around 1910, a Mr Bridge joined the firm, followed by Stanley Baron and

Following the merger, they became known simply as 'Campbells', and following the merger with Widdows Mason, for a short period became 'Widdows Campbell'.

The current partners and staff of Widdows Mason are proud of their history and traditions. Nonetheless, the business is modern, innovative and forward-thinking to meet the needs of 21st Century clients. Substantial investments in state-of-the-art computer and communications equipment have ensured the best of the past merges seamlessly with the best of the present.

This page: *The firms offices at High Street, Runcorn (top left) Westhoughton, Bolton (top right) and Arundel House, Rylands Street, Warrington.*

ACKNOWLEDGMENTS

The publishers would like to sincerely thank a number of individuals and organisations for their help and contribution to this publication.

This book would have been almost impossible without the kind co-operation of the following:

Ron Hunt

www.wiganworld.co.uk

Wigan Archives Service, WLCT

www.wlct.org/culture/heritage/archives.htm

All reasonable steps were taken by the publishers of this book to trace the copyright holders and obtain permission to use the photographs contained herein. However, due to the passage of time certain individuals were untraceable. Should any interested party subsequently come to light, the publishers can be contacted at the phone number printed at the front of this book and the appropriate arrangements will then be made.